A DAY IN THE LIFE OF GOD

MICHAEL DE-LA-NOY

THE AUTHOR

A DAY
IN THE LIFE
OF GOD

MICHAEL DE-LA-NOY

1971
THE CITADEL PRESS
DERBY

A Day In The Life of God
by Michael De-la-Noy
was first published in
February 1971 by
THE CITADEL PRESS
whose editorial offices are at
1 The Hill, Chellaston, Derby

This book
and all other publications of
The Citadel Press
are distributed to the book trade by
Tom Stacey Limited
28 Maiden Lane, London, W.C.2

Printed in Great Britain by
Keyworth and Fry Limited
Portland Street, Lincoln

C'est plus qu'un crime, c'est une faute: *Talleyrand*

CONTENTS

PREFACE

In 1967 I was appointed assistant information officer at the Church Information Office and press officer to the Archbishop of Canterbury. Within about twelve months of taking up these two appointments I was asked by a publisher if I would write a book about the Archbishop. I declined to do so while I was working for him. During the spring of 1970, however, I began to think about my future; by the autumn of 1970 I should have been working as a press officer for three years, and I thought it would by then be about time for me to return to journalism. But the Archbishop was due to undertake a tour of the Province of the Church of South Africa that November, and therefore I had in mind to remain in his service until the following spring, and then to offer to resign at his convenience.

With this tentative timetable in mind I contacted the publishers who had first approached me, and said I would now like to write a journalistic pen-portrait of the Archbishop, to be published some six months after my resignation. A contract was drawn up and I was about to begin work on the projected book when the whole course of my life was suddenly changed. I was sacked.

Clearly it became impossible to write the sort of book which originally I had had in mind. My immediate reaction was that I should in fact find it impossible to write a book at all, but as I began to see the situation more clearly, and as in any case events began to take on an even odder aspect than I could ever have imagined possible, I came to believe that a book was justified, and indeed was necessary; for the hamfisted manner in which I was sacked gave to the Church of England its worst publicity for years, and ultimate responsibility for this disaster lies, I believe, with those

1

who were, and I fear still are, anxious to see the ecclesiastical establishment function without any real regard for the age in which we live. My hope is that some effort will now be made to change this state of affairs.

The only really hard decision I have had to make was whether to publish the book while Dr. Michael Ramsey remained Archbishop of Canterbury. I have decided to do so because I believe the lessons of the debâcle through which the Church lived as a result of my dismissal need to be assimilated and acted upon before his successor is appointed.

I have received much help and encouragement in writing this book, as well as some discouragement! First I must thank the Archbishop of Canterbury for generously and courageously agreeing that I should paraphrase his private and confidential letter to me of 19th July, 1970. I am also grateful to the editors of *Forum* and *New Society* for giving me permission to reprint articles which appeared in their magazines. I have received much assistance over factual research from my friends and former colleagues Robert Whyte and Michael Jacob. Miss Elizabeth Baker, assistant secretary of the Department of International Affairs at the British Council of Churches, Mr. Geoffrey Moorhouse, Colonel Robert Hornby, the Reverend Adrian Esdaile, Mr. Jack Tinker and the BBC have also helped me. I am grateful for a lot of secretarial assistance from Miss Wendy Conway, and Colin Bostock-Smith has been kind enough to read and comment upon the manuscript. I wish I could thank Sir John Scott, the Archdeacon of Chester and Major-General Adam Block for agreeing to be interviewed in order to help me write a fair and accurate account of events with which they were intimately concerned, but all three have declined to see me. Happily, the hundreds of journalists, long-lost friends and complete strangers who took the trouble to telephone or write, expressing bewilderment and sympathy, taught me that the Church of England has more interested well-wishers and spectators, even though some of them may be in disguise, than it ever seems to realise.

For their love and hospitality when I most needed it I shall always be particularly grateful to Anne and Nicolas Stacey, Michael Carson, Jindra and Michael Burton, John Andrew and Nigel Curry.

MICHAEL DE-LA-NOY

2

CHAPTER ONE

THE CHURCH
BY LAW ESTABLISHED

There is no structural organisation of society which can bring about the coming of the Kingdom of God on earth, since all systems can be perverted by the selfishness of man:
William Temple.

WHEN I was sacked by the Church of England I took part in a drama far larger than the sum of the individual people concerned or the actual matter of my sacking. I was involved in the death throes of a dinosaur. What is interesting is that the extremis of the institutional Church should attract so much attention, and what is painful is that the institutional Church, like Charles II — once its polite and witty Supreme Governor — should be taking such an unconscionable time dying. I believe that much of the superficial interest still shown in almost anything the Church of England does can be traced back to the historical results of the Reformation, in essence to the fact that the Church of England is by law the established Church of this realm. While I also believe that the institutional Church is as cumbersome as a dinosaur, and should be eased as gently as possible into an honourable grave, I fear there are in fact many years of somewhat decayed life left in her. You simply do not unscramble overnight the organisational structures of something as rich, prestigious and deeply rooted in the life of the nation as a Church with the right to crown and annoint its sovereign, with 26 seats in the Upper House of Parliament, and as much capital to invest every twelve months as it is likely to take Oxfam or Shelter forty years to raise.

The reasons why the institutional Church resembles an animal hopelessly ill-equipped to survive in its environment will I hope emerge from this book. What I also hope will one day emerge, like the traditional phoenix, will be a Church in England unencumbered by insensitivity to the world it exists to serve. But spiritual reformation goes hand-in-hand with administrative competence, and a considerable effort of will is going to be needed by men and women whose complacency about the status quo can not be disguised for ever, even from themselves, if some good is to come out of evil; the specific evil to which I refer, the causes of which I believe to be symptomatic of so much that is wrong with the Church, occurred when through a succession of bizarre events leading to a final blunder compounded of breathtaking stupidity and a total lack of any intelligent appraisal of a potentially lethal situation, the Church of England, and in particular its senior primate, was made in the eyes of the world to look not only foolish and ill-informed about the facts of life, but positively un-Christian.

The characters and organisations, all of them part of the ecclesiastical establishment, who were involved in this fiasco are far from easy to pin down. As in other establishments, the Church establishment has its quota of shadowy figures who drop hints here, have words there, go about their lawful business in the Army and Navy Club, meet at weekend conferences, hunt, shoot and fish together, and work extremely hard in the intervals. Some have functions less easily defined than others; no one, for instance, questions the movements, all of them no doubt entirely proper, of the Archbishops' appointments secretary, who flits in truly Anglican style from diocese to diocese 'with his ear to the ground', 'taking soundings', just as the Conservative Party used to do, and who pops up at Lambeth Palace from time to time miraculously armed with the names of those next in line to the apostles.

Who actually constitute the 'establishment'? The question was once asked of me by a bishop from overseas, whom everybody was tipping for an English diocese. He and I went through a list of all those men who might reasonably be considered members of the Cabal, and the only trouble was that every single one of them had in recent weeks come up to the bishop and said, "You're staying on in England, of course. There must be a job for you here." When told by the bishop that he had heard nothing of that sort about his future, his well-wishers all replied, "Good heavens, I should have thought 'they' would have offered you something".

So in defining the 'establishment' one has to generalise. I would nominate for inclusion the 43 diocesan bishops, the three Church Estates Commissioners, the elected and ex-officio members of the General Synod, the senior officers of the General Synod, the secretaries of the boards and councils of the General Synod, and a small group of individual servants of the Church, for example, the Archbishop of Canterbury's senior chaplain, his lay assistant and his Registrar, the Archbishop of York's lay chaplain and the Archbishops' appointments secretary. Effective government is nearly always carried on by a minority of those elected to govern, and it is impossible to say just how many men effectively govern the Church of England. I think the criteria for effective membership of the establishment is whether you are actually able to influence decisions.

On that criteria by no means every diocesan bishop can be said to be an effective member of the establishment. There are plenty of diocesan bishops whose opinions are seldom sought on any topic, unless out of courtesy. I would say that the number of bishops who truly enjoy any real measure of the Archbishop of Canterbury's confidence number no more than three or four. In theory, the bishop closest to him is his senior chaplain, the Bishop of Maidstone, who is meant to share with Mr. Hugh Whitworth, the Archbishop's lay assistant, the sort of relationship to the Primate that Sir Michael Adeane has with the Queen. But in practice neither the Bishop of Maidstone nor Mr. Whitworth are necessarily consulated by the Archbishop on every important issue.

At the head of the secretariat in Church House is Sir John Guillum Scott, secretary of the General Synod.* The General Synod is the governing body of the Church of England. It constitutes its own boards and councils to carry out specific functions, and votes an annual budget for their work. There are of course clearly defined limits to Sir John's constitutional powers, but the extent of his personal influence over the secretaries of the boards and councils, over the members of the Synod and over the way in which the standing committee decides to handle the Synod's business is very considerable. His knowledge of Church law, standing orders and ecclesiastical events and personalities is probably unrivalled; so too

---

*Prior to November, 1970 the governing body of the Church of England was the Church Assembly. Its powers are now vested in the General Synod, and for the purposes of this book the two bodies will be treated as synonymous.

is his political instinct, and his natural caution. For all his apparent concern at the inability of the Synod to push ahead with reforms, and his professed despair at the tiresomely predictable antics of some of the members of the Synod, Sir John will definitely be listed on the day of judgment as a conservative.

And of course he is not the only conservative member of the establishment; liberals and radicals are at a considerable premium. The only senior bishop who at present could possibly be termed a liberal is the Bishop of Durham. There are 43 diocesan bishops, all virtually autonomous rulers in their own dioceses. The 26 bishops who at any one time sit in the House of Lords constitute the so-called bench of bishops. Seats in the House of Lords do not necessarily go to the most influential or intelligent bishops; the five senior bishops (Canterbury, York, London, Durham and Winchester) are all ex-officio members of the Lords. The remainder of the seats are given to the other 21 bishops as they achieve seniority by date of consecration.

The Church of England is divided into two provinces, each with its own archbishop. There is at the archiepiscopal see of York the opportunity for a prelate of stature to carve for himself a place in his own right in the life of the Church and nation. The see should never be regarded merely as a stepping stone to Canterbury. It is true that the present Archbishop of Canterbury was translated from York, but in retrospect his career from 1952, when he was consecrated to the senior bishopric of Durham, can be seen to have been planned by the establishment with the intention of leading him anyway to the throne of St. Augustine. But Archbishop Fisher went to Canterbury from London. William Temple, probably the greatest Archbishop of Canterbury this century, made his reputation at Manchester and York, and only held the see of Canterbury for two years. The present Archbishop of York's predecessor but one, Cyril Garbett, was an excellent example of a great archbishop who did not need to occupy the see of Canterbury at all in order to make a name for himself and to enhance the dignity of the northern province.

It can hardly be held by Dr. Donald Coggan's best friends that he has done anything to enhance the dignity of his province or to promote any major cause in the interests of Church or State since he was translated from Bradford to the see of York in 1961. It has been rumoured that Dr. Fisher wanted Dr. Coggan to go straight to Canterbury; it has also been assumed that his translation to York was a sop to the evangelicals, who were supposed to be feeling alarmed at the prospect of Michael Ramsey wafting incense all over the place.

As a biblical scholar Dr. Coggan has a deservedly high reputation, but in assessing pastoral situations he seems to many people incapable of applying any secular criteria; too often he appears merely content to look up the appropriate chapter and verse. Or else he puts his foot in it by tasteless remarks which cause offence to the very people he is charged to help. He once referred to young couples who have sex before marriage as second-hand goods. Despite severe criticism over that, he managed, in Meeting Point in January, 1962 to patronise Adam Faith in one of the most embarrassing television programmes ever devised, and when, three years later, on 21st June, 1965 he spoke in public about the media on which he had acquitted himself so badly he saw fit to refer to the "gormless millions" who watch it.

This happened before I had any idea I would ever be elected a member of Church Assembly, or ever dreamt that one day I should be press officer to the Archbishop of Canterbury. So, alas perhaps for my own future career, I wrote to the Archbishop of York asking him to take greater care in future over his use of language. I received the most astonishing reply. Dr. Coggan said he naturally regretted any offence his remarks may have caused, but he asked me to forgive him on the grounds that he had not known what gormless meant! How a man can be Bishop of Bradford for five years and not know what gormless means defeats me, and if he did not know what the word meant what on earth was he doing using it?

Dr. Coggan's apparent lack of understanding about public relations is shared by an alarming number of the other bishops. Few are as tactless as Dr. Coggan, but few could be said to care for the press, or to have any innate sympathy for means of communication more modern than the sermon. There are one or two, like the Bishop of Bristol and the Bishop of Hereford, who have made efforts to understand what television is all about, but the depth of ignorance the bishops display about the sort of relationship the Church should have with the press is lamentable. Dr. Launcelot Fleming of Norwich is one of the few bishops who at least understands the first principle, that public relations is a professional extension of personal relations; as a result, his house and his tele-

7

phone number are by-words for courtesy and commonsense in the news room of television companies and newspaper offices in East Anglia. Dr. Ian Ramsey, the Bishop of Durham, also has soundly-based relations with his local newspapers; no matter how busy he is, and he is often too busy, he will prepare a statement under pressure, which may tend to be too long, but at least shows a proper concern about the subject. But too many bishops still think the appropriate comment is always "no comment", and the Bishop of London actually boasts that he gets his wife to answer the telephone, and if it is the press, she is told to say as a matter of course that he is out.

London is the senior bishopric after the two archbishoprics. Again, London is a see made famous in the past by men who have gone no further up the ladder. One thinks of Bishop Winnington-Ingram. But future generations are unlikely to remember the name of the present bishop, Dr. Robert Stopford. In 1961 Dr. Stopford was Bishop of Peterborough and was tipped, at safe odds, for Canterbury. He has made his mark primarily in education. He is a solid, dependable sort of figure, but with nothing about his presence or his voice that could ever be described as exciting. He rules an impossible diocese, in which the suffragan-bishops are now virtually diocesans in all but name; it is a diocese that calls for flair and imagination, two characteristics the Bishop simply does not have. Few of his major appointments have been inspired, and all in all I would say that if the image of the establishment nobly but boringly propping up a tottering edifice can be focused on one man, it can, fairly or unfairly, be focused on Robert Stopford.

Historically, the other two bishoprics to rank as 'senior' are Durham and Winchester. To be consecrated to Durham is a measure of your stature at the start of the episcopal stakes. It is a strange coincidence that the present Bishop of Durham, Dr. Ian Ramsey, should be the namesake but in no way the relation of the present Archbishop of Canterbury; both were consecrated to Durham, and by general consent both stand intellectually head and shoulders above their episcopal contempories. Michael Ramsey was Regius Professor of Divinity at Cambridge; Ian Ramsey was Nolloth Professor of the Philosophy of the Christian Religion at Oxford. He is the only bishop being tipped as Michael Ramsey's successor. The Archbishop is known to regard Ian Ramsey's pastoral gifts as well as his intellectual attainments with satisfaction, although in the event of his retirement from Canterbury it is by no means certain that he will be consulted about his successor. Dr. Fisher was not consulted when he resigned. Not only is Ian Ramsey being tipped by the Church for eventual translation to Canterbury, he is almost the only diocesan bishop who has made any impact in the country in recent years. The truth of the matter is that only Canterbury, Durham, Southwark, Trevor Huddleston (now Bishop of Stepney), David Sheppard (now Bishop of Woolwich) and John Robinson (formerly bishop of Woolwich and now Dean of Trinity College, Cambridge) are anything resembling household names.

Of the other senior members of the bench, nothing enlightening can be said of Dr. Falkner Allison, Bishop of Winchester. The reputation of Dr. Oliver Tomkins of Bristol rests mainly on his ecumenical activities; he is listened to in the General Synod with respect rather than interest, and some of the radical members tend to suspect the facade he can adopt of a wounded spaniel. The Bishop of Chester, Dr. Gerald Ellison, was I believe the youngest bishop in the Church of England when he was consecrated to the suffragan-bishopric of Willesden in 1950. He has been at Chester since 1955 and is thought to have a hopeful eye on London. He started the Boat Race the year one of the boats sank. His ecumenical sympathies may not be all that sympathetic, and he tends to worry about such trivia as whether or not people call him Father. He also once gave the blessing at the launching of a Polaris submarine, so he too is not very popular among the radicals.

Nepotism is at a healthy premium in the Church of England, and I think the Bishop of Chichester, Dr. Roger Wilson, who was another of the Church's bright young men when he was consecrated to the diocesan bishopric of Wakefield at the age of 44, is the only bishop related to another, in fact to the Archbishop of Canterbury. They are cousins. Dr. Wilson seems to have little of the personal touch in his sprawling diocese, but he is certainly sound on international affairs, in the liberal tradition of his great predecessor, George Bell.

The Bishop of Coventry, Dr. Cuthbert Bardsley, always reminds me of the Queen Mother, for both appear to be good at their jobs because both so obviously enjoy them. Dr. Bardsley is very Anglican, a sort of do-it-yourself catholic-evangelical. While he is exhorting you to go to confession you almost expect him to ask if you are saved. He is certainly the only bishop who at present

9

understands anything about mission, a much maligned and misunderstood activity. Whatever your emotional response to the rallies and missions Dr. Bardsley conducts you have to hand it to him, he certainly knows how to pack 'em in, even if he does not exactly speak to the modern generation.

Dr. Robert Mortimer has held the see of Exeter since 1949. He is an autocrat, a prince-bishop of the old school, not the sort of man you would lightly telephone on a Saturday afternoon. He even gives the impression of walking apart from his fellow bishops. But he is a moral theologian of renown, and when he speaks in the General Synod he commands respect and attention.

Dr. Ronald Williams has been bishop of Leicester since 1953. He was an examining chaplain to Dr. Michael Ramsey when he was bishop of Durham. He started out in life rather more to the left than he has ended up, and is now defensive enough to have written a book called "What's Right with the Church of England". He was one of the five bishops who voted, in July 1968, against Anglican-Methodist reunion, and the speech he made during the final debate was so incompetent that it could only be accounted for by his personal distress at having to vote against a scheme so strongly backed by his friend the Archbishop. His attitude to the press is often distressingly typical of the bishops in general; at a period when *The Times* was fighting for its life all that seemed to worry Dr. Williams was the size of the type used for the Church announcements. And yet Dr. Williams is equally capable of seizing the initiative through an act of generosity. When *The Times* ran a feature on the Church in Leicester they made complete nonsense of a caption, the sort of mistake that causes the conscientious *Times* editorial staff to contemplate mass hari kari. On this occasion the Bishop, who was closely involved, declined any correction on the grounds that he thought *The Times* still deserved credit for their initiative in running the feature, and he did not wish to disturb the goodwill built up.

Perhaps the most right-wing bishop around at present is Dr. Stretton Reeve of Lichfield, who was consecrated the same year as Dr. Williams. It was thought by the Board for Social Responsibility a subtle move to appoint him chairman of a group set up to advise the Archbishop of Canterbury on the theological implications of the Wolfenden proposals affecting male homosexuality. The subtlety of the move was somewhat lost on the other members of the group, who spent many precious months educating their chairman in attitudes already adopted by most informed men of goodwill some ten years before.

Of the remaining 32 diocesans, mention might be made of the Bishop of Ripon, Dr. John Moorman, whose interests seem to lie almost exclusively in the direction of reunion with the Church of Rome, and who voted against Anglican-Methodist reunion. He gives the impression of being a rigid man, with little warmth, but perhaps he is shy. The Bishop of St. Edmundsbury and Ipswich is the only current example among the English diocesans of a bishop called in from overseas; he was formerly Archbishop of Uganda. He has brought to the Church of England a professed impatience with the pace of events and a dislike of the established system, but he shows little sign of blazing any new trails. The Bishop of Salisbury, Dr. Joseph Fison, consecrated in 1963, must be counted one of the significant episcopal appointments of recent times. He held the famous living of Great St. Mary's, Cambridge, which has produced two other bishops in recent years, Mervyn Stockwood of Southwark and Hugh Montefiore of Kingston-upon-Thames. He is an intellectual, which is rare among the bishops at present, and he is a cultured man with some knowledge of literature; I am sure it was right to make him a bishop but I doubt whether Salisbury was the right diocese.

Then there is the intrepid Dr. Stockwood of Southwark, who probably has as many friends as he has enemies. He is known outside the Church for his interest in most liberal causes and his membership of the Labour Party. Within the Church he is equally well known for his egocentricity and a certain pastoral insensitivity. It is true he has learnt some painful lessons from early mistakes; he made a great fuss shortly after becoming a bishop over a parish priest who was reserving the sacrament illegally, and I doubt whether he would be so foolish now as to take over the man's vestry and hold an impromptu press conference. But his reputation for running the most radical diocese in the Church of England rests on a few first-rate appointments made many years ago. Most of the stars have now left and the Southwark diocese is run today by men who have stuck themselves into tough if not intractible jobs. The Bishop meanwhile has gone ex-directory.

In making strictures on the Church's Fathers-in-God I have to remind myself that beneath their veneer of pomp they are generally

11

courteous men, even though there is only one diocesan bishop who has ever brought himself to invite me to address him by his Christian name. When the Bishop of Chester blessed his Polaris submarine I was then a member of the Church Assembly, and not an employee of the Church, and I sent him a telegram asking him to change his mind. I never expected the telegram would in fact cause the Bishop to alter his plans, but I never expected either that it would prompt him to write me a four-page letter in his own hand explaining his point of view. It is said by friends of the Archbishop of York that he is without pomposity of any kind. And, of course, beneath the copes and mitres quite often lie deep layers of insecurity, and in some cases even the scars of severe personal tragedies.

It is in the appointment of the bishops and deans that the two establishments, Church and State, meet most intimately. The Church of England, the mother Church of the Anglican Communion, is the only Church within the Communion that has its bishops appointed by the State; all the other Churches elect their own leaders. In principle, it can hardly be denied that an electoral system is right and proper, or at any rate that if the bishops are to be appointed they should be appointed by the Church. But not all electoral systems work well, and there are disadvantages inherent in most. What is probably needed in England is an electoral college with lay and clerical representatives from both the diocese in which the vacancy occurs and the Church at large.

At present however the English bishops are appointed by the Queen on the advice of the Prime Minister. This means that the Archbishops' and the Prime Minister's appointments secretaries work together to sift and nominate names; the actual process whereby the names go to the two archbishops and the Prime Minister remains a matter of conjecture. There are probably variations in the system; whether the Archbishop of York is always consulted over the appointment of diocesan bishops to the southern province I do not know, but I imagine he is. If the two archbishops do not share responsibility for the building up of the episcopal strength of the Church it is hard to imagine what they do share. In the case of appointments to suffragan-bishoprics it is almost certain that the diocesan bishop to whose see the appointment is going to be made is consulted, and he may even be invited to submit a name. It is after all unthinkable that a diocesan should have thrust upon him, to share his episcopate, a man of whom he disapproved or whom he actively disliked.

I think it must be assumed that no nomination for a bishopric would get as far as the Prime Minister's desk unless it had the blessing of the Archbishop of Canterbury, and presumably in the case of a nomination to the northern province of the Archbishop of York too, for after all these are the men who are going to consecrate. Just how much influence is ever directly exercised by the Prime Minister of the day is a matter for speculation. I find it perfectly feasible that if the Prime Minister happened to take a genuine interest in Church appointments he might discuss them with the Archbishop of Canterbury, or at least communicate his ideas to Lambeth Palace via his own appointments secretary, but I find it equally unlikely that he would ever actually wish to cross swords with the Archbishop of Canterbury, unless he really thought some projected appointment would be disastrous or immoral.

As for the Queen, I think it can reasonably be assumed that whereas she takes a keen personal interest in the name of the nominee placed before her, and will brief herself about the man if she does not already know him, she would never actually contemplate refusing to send his name to the dean and chapter of the diocese for the farcical ceremony of election. If the dean and chapter were to refuse to elect, or if the archbishops were to refuse to consecrate the sovereign's nominee, then I seem to remember they all get packed off to the Tower of London, but by this stage we have reached the realm of fairyland.

I do not doubt that the Archbishop's appointments secretary, Mr. William Saumarez Smith (who like Sir Ronald Harris of the Church Commissioners and Mr. Hugh Whitworth has been a member of the Indian Civil Service) takes the traditional soundings from a wide spectrum of Church life, although you will never actually meet anyone, other than a diocesan bishop, who will admit that one day over coffee during a break in Church Assembly Mr. Saumarez Smith came up to him and asked who he thought should be the new bishop of somewhere or other. My guess is that he works more discreetly and subtly than that, listening rather than talking, simply getting the feel of the Church, assessing the needs of a particular diocese, keeping mental tabs on potential episcopal material, and that in the end it is Mr. Saumarez Smith's personal judgment that produces the names that go to the Archbishop of Canterbury. If this assessment of the situation is accurate it makes Mr. Saumarez Smith one of the most powerful and influential men in the Church.

There are however a handful of laymen who are almost certainly consulted by Mr. Saumarez Smith. Sir John Scott's opinions must surely be sought. So must the chairman of the House of Laity, and the Archbishop of Canterbury's Registrar, Mr. David Carey, who advises the Archbishop on any legal matters, and is regarded as a member of his personal household. I know of one appointment to a particularly important suffragan-bishopric where Mr. Carey was totally instrumental in achieving promotion for a man he regarded as ideal for the post. In the northern province it must be assumed that Mr. Saumarez Smith keeps in close touch with the Archbishop of York's lay chaplain, Mr. David Blunt, a son of Bishop Blunt, who let the cat out of the bag over Mrs. Simpson. Mr. Blunt is a gentle and friendly man. In theory he should be an influential member of the establishment, but my impression is that he is more of an efficient and loyal secretary than a thrusting courtier.

There is a fairly clearly defined division of responsibility at Lambeth Palace between the Archbishop of Canterbury's senior chaplain and his lay assistant, although obviously much of their work overlaps. On the whole, the senior chaplain looks after specifically Church affairs, concerns himself with theological matters, acts as secretary to the bishops' meetings and is intended as a bridge builder between the Archbishop and the diocesan bishops. He tends to be consulted over pastoral matters. The lay assistant takes care of State affairs, House of Lords debates and the Archbishop's involvement in secular legislation and social reform. The appointment of a chaplain specifically described as 'senior' is fairly recent, and came about following the resignation of the Reverend John Andrew, who had been senior chaplain to the present Archbishop in all but name for eight years. John Andrew was a self-confessed courtier, a post for which he possessed many gifts, but he was considered by most of the bishops too young to act in any real way as a confidant. The present senior chaplain was archdeacon of Portsmouth when he was selected for the job, and he was consecrated to the suffragan-bishopric of Maidstone within the Canterbury diocese in order to give him an equal status with those senior clergy with whom he would be in confidential communication. For the first fourteen years of his ministry he was a naval chaplain, which may not have helped kindle particularly warm attitudes towards certain aspects of the modern world. He has a wary approach, and once told me that the press were like a pack of ravening wolves seeking whom they may devour. As a statement of fact it was I felt more colourful than accurate, and as a generalised description of a good many of my personal friends and colleagues it could perhaps have been more tactfully put.

The present Archbishop also has a domestic chaplain, who looks after the affairs of the Canterbury diocese, lives as a bachelor at the Palace, travels almost everywhere with the Archbishop, attends him at ecclesiastical ceremonies, breakfasts and lunches with the Archbishop and Mrs. Ramsey and acts as an equerry and an aide de camp. Officially his influence is small; he is liable to be a young priest, probably ordained only about three years, who would expect to serve for about three years in the post. In fact, because he lives so closely with the Archbishop and his wife, both in London and Canterbury, he probably gets to know them more intimately than the senior chaplain, who is married and lives in his own flat at Lambeth, and he has a serious responsibility to smooth the Archbishop's path and cheer him up, if need be, without actually wrapping him in cotton wool.

The Archbishop's lay assistant, Mr. Hugh Whitworth, is a former civil servant who has brought to his new job the natural caution of a public employee, but whose outlook is also genial and flexible. He had the difficult task in 1969 of succeeding Mr. Robert Beloe, one of the Church of England's great lay servants, who had held the post of secretary to the Archbishop of Canterbury since the last year of Dr. Fisher's incumbency. On Mr. Beloe's retirement the post was renamed, for reasons which remain obscure, and some of the responsibilities prevously undertaken by Mr. Beloe were transferred to the new senior chaplain. There is no doubt that Mr. Beloe's devoted service to Dr. Ramsey and the Church went largely unappreciated, and in dismantling the area of Mr. Beloe's operations the establishment may well have left Mr. Whitworth in too nebulous a position to exercise much initiative; after a year in the job he was still meeting diocesan bishops for the first time.

I would say that the members of the General Synod are all members of the establishment because they do have the opportunity of influencing decisions made by what is in fact the ultimate decision-making body of the Church; the Synod can make almost any decision it likes, affecting worship, work and doctrine. Its legislation must still go to Parliament for ratification, but a major political clash nowadays would be more likely to hasten disestablishment rather than prove a permanent setback for any important ecclesiastical policy. But within the Synod it is impossible to say definitely who wields the most significant influence. Obviously a minority of members are more influential than others, and the members of the standing committee are probably the most influential of all.

The Synod is more than a microcosm of the Church, it is a focal point for the dual nature of the Church of England, part democratic part authoritarian, in which the diocesan bishops sit as a separate House, as ex-officio members of a Synod containing predominantly elected representatives of the clergy and laity. The Church seems content that their Fathers-in-God should be there as of right, because in the bishops the Church believes there resides a responsibility to teach the gospel and defend the Faith. Yet the Synod also sets equal store by the newly acquired right of the laity to debate and vote on matters of doctrine, as the absolute equals, on these occasions, of the bishops and clergy, to whom in matters liturgical however they still play a very secondary rôle.

In the old Church Assembly retired army officers and titled ladies and gentlemen of one sort or another flourished. I do not believe a title should necessarily bar you from public service; the Earl of March is a good example of a young and extremely hard-working member of the upper crust who may well be driven to excessive zeal through feelings of guilt about his privileged position in society, but whose talents and concerns are very real. Nevertheless, the image given by the House of Laity of the Tory Party at prayer is, and is likely to remain, an unmistakable one.

It is in the General Synod as well as in the House of Lords that Church and State can most clearly be seen to meet. In the House of Laity of the old Church Assembly there were four members of Parliament together with two peers in addition to Lord March, who is not a peer of the realm. The House also contained six baronets, eight knights, a major-general, two brigadiers, a naval captain, six commanders, a group captain, no less than 14 colonels, four majors and three army captains.

The scramble for seats at the elections in September, 1970 for the new General Synod was astonishing. The size of the Synod has been reduced considerably, from 693 elective seats to around 500, yet some 2,500 priests and lay men and women tried to get in. In the result, many well-known and useful members fell by the wayside, and about half the House of Laity were elected for the first time and perhaps some two-thirds of the House of Clergy.

Voting patterns throughout the country varied enormously. While rejecting Miss Valerie Pitt, apparently on the grounds that she was not radical enough, which was not for want of trying, the Southwark diocese still managed to send back the most exciting list of candidates, including Canon Eric James, who seems to have the enviable ability to rock boats without ever actually upsetting them, the Reverend Paul Oestreicher, who should keep the Synod's conscience awake on international issues, Mr. Robert Beloe and Miss Priscilla Cornwall-Jones, who is tipped to take over the mantle of radicalism from Miss Pitt.

The roll-call included Mr. Timothy Royal, a young and energetic evangelical who failed to get back for Coventry, the Reverend Eddy Stride, an astringent proctor for Chelmsford, who used to keep the old Church Assembly high up on its toes, Canon Bernard Pawley, a witty radical, who knew and cared a great deal about ecumenical affairs, and the Reverend Percy Coleman, chaplain-extraordinary to the Anglo-Catholics.

Apart from its reduction in size, the main difference between the new General Synod and the old Church Assembly is that the laity will have an equal say with the bishops and clergy on matters of doctrine. Whether the life of the Church will improve as a result remains to be seen. The most influential body within the Synod will continue to be the Standing Committee, who decide the business of the Synod and give special time to debates which they feel should have priority. Their influence is obviously considerable, but in the end they can only set plans in motion; it is the unpredictable and indefinable spirit of the Synod that breathes life into or squeezes life out of the best or worst intentions of its own Standing Committee and its own civil service.

The civil service is concentrated in Church House, an ugly mid-war building in Dean's Yard, built around the debating chamber where three times a year the Synod's employees crowd into the galleries or sit behind the rostrum to hear debates affecting their work, and sometimes their livelihood. There are a dozen boards and councils answerable to the General Synod, divided into some 22 separate departments. The budget voted annually for their work is now over £1 million.

The Central Board of Finance administers the budget, and acts as a general treasury for the other boards and councils. The Advisory Council for the Church's Ministry is responsible for recruiting ordinands, and also runs a council for the ministry of women. The Board of Education, the Missionary and Ecumenical Council, the Board for Social Responsibility and the Church Information Office are the other major boards and councils. There is also a Legal Board, a Council for the Care of Churches, a Council for Commonwealth Settlement, a Council for the Deaf, and Hospital and Prison Chaplaincy Councils.

The Church Commissioners constitute perhaps the most complex component of the ecclesiastical establishment. It is necessary to be a financial wizard to understand the Commissioners' finances and an ecclesiastical politician to take on the task of challenging their policies. At the head of the Commissioners is Sir Ronald Harris, whose title of First Church Estates Commissioner is itself sufficient to surround him in an atmosphere of awe. Sir Ronald was formerly a civil servant. He is a personable and youngish-looking man, wealthy himself and obviously far from shy about spending £23 millions a year of the Church's money.

The Commissioners came into being in 1948 when an 18th century invention called Queen Anne's Bounty was merged with a 19th century creation called the Ecclesiastical Commissioners. The relationship between the Commissioners and the General Synod is far from clear, except that all the 43 diocesan bishops are Commissioners, together with 25 clergy and laity nominated by the Synod. By and large the Commissioners finance about three-quarters of the clergy stipends, contribute towards clergy and clergy widow pensions, and look after clergy houses. They own farming land and domestic property but realise the majority of their income from stocks and shares.

The Commissioners' secular affiliations afford a fascinating example of the Church of England's seemingly insatiable ties with the State. The following Gilbertian entourage are members: the Lord Chancellor, the Lord President of the Council, the First Lord of the Treasury, the Chancellor of the Exchequer, the Secretary of State for the Home Department, the Speaker of the House of Commons, the Lord Chief Justice, the Master of the Rolls, the Attorney-General, the Solicitor-General, the Lord Mayor of

London, the Lord Mayor of York, and nominees of the Court of Aldermen and the Universities of Oxford and Cambridge. None of these worthy gentlemen need be Christians, let alone Anglicans.

According to *The Church of England Year Book*, "The full body of the Commissioners normally meets once a year to consider the Reports and Accounts which are then transmitted to Parliament and the Church Assembly and published, and the allocation of available money." On these annual occasions the Commissioners issue from their offices in Millbank the shortest possible press release offering the minimum information about their current affairs. They then sit down to an excellent lunch in the Guard Room at Lambeth Palace.

CHAPTER TWO

THE SEE OF CAUNTERBURIE

*Through the years of my priesthood the paradox has more and
more come home to me: the paradox that divine power and love, the
resources of Heaven itself, can use, and use not in vain, wayward,
sinful human nature like our own:*   Michael Ramsey.

THE Guard Room at Lambeth Palace, the London home of the
Archbishop of Canterbury, is situated in a house that is far from
beautiful but to many people almost represents the beatific vision.
It is not really surprising that an institution historically as entrenched as the Church of England yet in many ways apparently
so undisciplined should have acquired, and should still require, a
focal point. For the Church of England itself, for the Anglican
Communion, for Churches outside the Anglican Communion and
for the nation that focal point is the see of Canterbury. For many
people, the see of Canterbury *is* the Church of England, the Church
of England *is* the Anglican Communion, and the current occupant
of St. Augustine's throne is the universal father figure to whom the
press will automatically turn for comment on moral issues, upon
whom the Church will lazily lean for leadership, and with whom
city bankers and agnostic politicians, in search of a talisman for
their nefarious activities, will always be anxious to dine.

The briefest glance at history will explain the emergence of
Canterbury as the dominant diocese in the Anglican Church. The
see was founded by St. Augustine, who while he may not actually
have been the first Christian to set foot on English soil was certainly
the first to become an archbishop. After an unseemly tussle between
Canterbury and York (at one time the servants of the two archbishops came to blows, and Canterbury's lot sat firmly on the

21

stomach of the Archbishop of York, and therefore reckoned they had won) the southern province established its supremacy. As senior primate in the Church of England, the Archbishop of Canterbury claimed the right to annoint and crown the sovereign, and in mediaeval England the Church virtually ruled the land alongside the king, offering promises of paradise in return for taxes paid today, and promises of hell in case of default. At the time of the Reformation the Church became not less powerful, but in many ways more so, for while it is true that the Church lost much of its astronomical wealth and a good deal of its freedom to order its own way of life, by acquiring the sovereign as Supreme Governor and having its affairs regulated by secular law it gained in prestige, and continues to gain in prestige as secularism overtakes religiosity, far more than it lost in political power. It is primarily on the simple basis of prestige that today the see of Canterbury exerts, or fails to exert, influence on the life both of Church and State.

As far as the Church of England is concerned, the Archbishop of Canterbury exercises an overall pastoral care of the diocesan bishops in his own province, acts as archbishop to half-a-dozen extra-provincial dioceses overseas, sits as joint president of the General Synod and is chairman of the Church Commissioners. Whether the present Archbishop's lay assistant has, posted up anywhere, a definitive list of committees and organisations with which the Archbishop is connected, as chairman, patron or visitor, I do not know, but if he has it must cover several decent-sized drawing boards.

It is perhaps through the administrative and legal work of the General Synod that the Archbishop physically spends most time attempting to foster the parochial life of the Church, and the Archbishop's responsibility to the General Synod alone involves him in endless, and very often boring, hours of reading, thought and the preparation of appropriate action, some of which gets translated into speeches, still more of which forms the basis of interviews with the Archbishop of York, the secretary of the General Synod, the chairmen of the Houses of Clergy and Laity and his Registrar. It is no secret that the present Archbishop, unlike his predecessor Dr. Fisher, finds the work of the General Synod the least creative and the least personally rewarding of all the duties he has to undertake. His grasp of standing orders is minimal, which in itself is no great handicap, as the secretary is always by his side to see fair play, but it is indicative of the personality of the Archbishop; standing orders bore him, so they have no place in his mind. Dr. Ramsey is actually capable of wishing that something like standing orders did not exist to the point that for him they more or less don't.

It is impossible to be a really effective chairman of a body whose activities do not intrinsically hold your interest, and Dr. Ramsey's reputation is unlikely to rest on his chairmanship of the old Church Assembly. It is a blessing that under the rules of the new General Synod there will be a panel of chairmen, to whom Dr. Ramsey can certainly be counted on to hand over the chair with a good grace. He will still however be involved in an endless succession of committees, whose purpose may well be to streamline the work of the Synod when it meets in full session, but whose existence will do nothing to set the Archbishop free to pursue activities more suited to his own particular aptitudes.

In the life of the nation, the see of Canterbury quite simply epitomises the spiritual links that every man, woman and child possesses with the Church of their fathers, and which few would wish to see abolished, however seldom they may in fact avail themselves of the comforts of religion. Part of the reason for the Archbishop's prominence in the collective conscientiousness is the privileged position afforded him by the established status of the Church. He ranks in the hierarchy immediately after the Royal Family; while the diocesan bishops rank only as barons the Archbishop of Canterbury is regarded as a duke, and he takes precedence as the first commoner in the land. He is addressed as "Your Grace", lives in a couple of palaces, is automatically sworn in a member of the Privy Council, acts as chief pastor to the Royal Family, and even presents visiting cardinals to the Queen while the Archbishop of Westminster stays at home.

He is also keeper of the nation's conscience. When moral issues raise their heads it is to the Archbishop of Canterbury that the press and radio first turn for comment. A controversial comment is never unwelcome, but what most people most often want is a word of reassurance. They want to be told that in a changing and bewildering world the laws of God don't change, and if they can be told how to apply those laws to changing circumstances without being told to go to too much inconvenience, so much the better. And if they can get all this free advice from the top man, it is usually regarded as valid. But while the Archbishop is keeper of the nation's conscience it also behoves him to behave in a way that accords with the nation's hypocritical attitudes towards its leaders. In the case of politicians, once every five years the electorate abdicates personal responsibility by electing parliamentary candidates to take decisions and actions for them, reserving the right to round on their generally hard-working, underpaid and ludicrously ill-equipped members of Parliament whenever they feel decisions are not being taken exclusively in their own interests. In the case of the Archbishop, the situation is even more hypocritical, for whereas most people are at least political to the extent that they vote, if the Archbishop appears to be violating some sacred remnant of tradition he is liable to find himself serving as a whipping boy for the discontents of millions of men and women who have previously paid no heed whatsoever to the Church or its teachings. He may even find himself in this position without so much as opening his mouth, for there is a sense in which people expect their spiritual leaders to wave a magic wand once or twice a week, to keep the old order in sound repair. If standards seem to be slipping, if mini-skirts are getting too short or too many black men are entering the country, or too few for that matter, the Archbishop is as good a person as any to take a bit of the blame; it is generally felt that he ought to be 'doing something about it'. There are some fairly clear naturally prescribed limits to the Archbishop's actual ability to do something about a whole lot of things. These are in themselves of considerable interest. What is even more fascinating are the abstract areas in which the Archbishop may, or may no longer, wield a powerful, indirect influence on the quality of our life.

In addition to his duties to the Church of England, to his own diocese and to the State through his membership of the House of Lords, the present Archbishop undertakes a good many tasks as a result of his personal concern for closer relations with other Churches. For six years he served as a president of the World Council of Churches. This involved him in committee work as well as visits to New Delhi and Uppsala for meetings of the Third and Fourth Assemblies. At home the Archbishop is president of the British Council of Churches, and chairs their three-day meetings twice a year. Hardly a year goes past without the Archbishop receiving an Orthodox Patriarch at Lambeth or Canterbury, usually for a visit of about three days. Every year the Archbishop receives the Moderator

24

At Easter, 1968, the Archbishop gave an interview at the Old Palace, Canterbury, to Arthur Helliwell of *The People*, whose photographer caught him in a pose many journalists will be quick to recognise.

This is the benign and fatherly archbishop whose presence is revered throughout the overseas Churches of the Anglican Communion. The Archbishop had just preached at a service in Christ Church Cathedral, Nassau, on the first Sunday of his 1968 tour of the Church of the Province of the West Indies.

Photograph by Stanley Toogood

of the General Assembly of the Church of Scotland, and he is the first Archbishop of Canterbury to have been invited to address the General Assembly. He is in constant touch with the leaders of the Roman Catholic Church in this country and overseas, and maintains permanent personal links with the Vatican. The Council on Foreign Relations, with offices in the grounds of Lambeth Palace, acts as a Foreign Office to the Archbishop, keeping him in contact with Churches outside the Anglican Communion and with overseas governments.

Dr. Ramsey is far and away the most widely travelled holder of his office. His ecumenical adventures have taken him to Moscow, Constantinople, Athens, Louvain, Roumania, Rome, Belgrade, Geneva, Bec and Paris. As a result of his visits to Churches of the Anglican Communion his personal knowledge of the Commonwealth is probably only rivalled by the Queen's. He has been to Canada, Nigeria, New Zealand, Australia, Honululu and Fiji, Mauritius and Madagascar, Bermuda and the West Indies, and outside the Commonwealth he has paid visits to West Germany, Puerto Rico, the United States of America, South Africa and Uganda.

Finally, there is the relationship of the see of Canterbury to the Anglican Communion. There are now 19 separate Churches or Provinces in the Communion, all in communion with the see of Canterbury but all autonomous. The bishops of the Communion meet at Lambeth every ten years, at the personal invitation of the Archbishop of Canterbury, but as president of the Lambeth Conference the Archbishop is merely first among equals. The present Archbishop can seldom have been happier than when presiding over the Conference of 1968. Intellectually he towered head and shoulders over his fellow primates, and he captivated all the bishops by his linguistic lucidity, his humour and his innate sensitivity to the loosely-knit nature of the Conference.

What established the supremacy of the see of Canterbury in the eyes of the Anglican Church overseas was its antiquity and its position as the archiepiscopal diocese from which the Anglican Church sent missionaries to the rest of the world. What has kept Canterbury in the affections of the Anglican Church has largely been a colonial nostalgia for England. Whether Canterbury will continue to remain the focal point of the Anglican Communion remains to be seen. I think it very possible that the 1978 Lambeth Conference will take place in the U.S.A. or Africa, even though the Archbishop of Canterbury may still take the chair. But as each Church continues to take unilateral action on matters like the ordination of women and intercommunion it seems to me there is no guarantee that the basis for the Conference, communion with the see of Canterbury, will in fact be able to remain intact.

It is hard to define exactly the kind of leadership the Church of England expects from its senior primate, and one would like to think that the Church would adjust its demands in the light of each archbishop's particular interests and capabilities. But in some respect or other I suppose the Church always expects a degree of scholarship. What the Church has failed to do is to see that time is set aside for the Archbishop of Canterbury to place his scholastic abilities at the service of the community. Few people have any conception of the load of work that awaits the Archbishop each day. The present Archbishop likes to receive an invitation each year or 18 months to visit a Church of the Anglican Communion overseas, in addition to any specifically ecumenical visit he may be planning, and the amount of preparation for a three weeks' visit to the Church of the Province of the West Indies, or to the United States, or to the Church of the Province of South Africa, with perhaps twenty sermons to prepare, half-a-dozen theological lectures, and a dozen speeches at schools, universities, theological colleges and dinners, takes an enormous amount of time, time which has to be taken out of the daily routine at home.

In Holy Week in 1970 Dr. Ramsey gave three lectures in New York to bishops of the Episcopal Church in the U.S.A., on "The Future of the Christian Church." He also gave a public lecture on the same subject, which was televised. Those lectures then had to be corrected for publication in a book. This is the sort of task that a university don might find strenuous, whose entire life is given up to teaching. For the Archbishop, the preparation of these lectures had to be undertaken while doing five or six other jobs at the same time. And yet I am quite sure it is right that any Archbishop of Canterbury should be placing his thoughts on the most vital issues of the day before the Church and society; the solution to his work load almost certainly lies in the delegation of other duties, particularly among the bishops.

There has until very recently been a desire, and I think a natural one, to approach the Archbishop of Canterbury for comment on almost any subject of national interest, and to treat him as an

26

automatic expert on almost every subject. In the past two or three years attempts have been made to deflect responsibility for statements on certain issues to other senior and particularly knowledgeable bishops. For example, the Bishop of Durham is now regarded as the Church's unofficial spokesman on transplant operations. This is a desirable trend, when so many modern techniques in scientific fields give rise to ethical issues that need the most careful study. Dr. Michael Ramsey was perfectly happy to take on reform of the law affecting male homosexuality, the abolition of hanging and the integration of Commonwealth immigrants. He could well have done without making himself into an expert on abortion and divorce law reform as well. I suspect that had he specifically asked one or two of the other bishops to take over the social subjects he felt he would prefer not to cope with entirely on his own, with the co-operation of the Church Information Office something of the presidential system under which Dr. Ramsey works could quite easily have been broken down before now. But the fact remains there is a seeming lack of volunteers among the bishops for these sort of extra-curricular activities.

What all this amounts to is that so long as Lambeth Palace remains staffed a great deal less adequately than it should be the present tasks undertaken by the Archbishop of Canterbury are too much for any one man to carry out properly, particularly if he is to undertake any original scholarship and to write books while in office, and more important still if he is to take a broad view of the needs of the Church and the nation during his time at Canterbury, and to map out a plan of campaign, based on his probable term of office and an order of priorities regarding the current life of the Church and nation. What any archbishop will find himself doing in the present situation is running fast in order to keep in the same position. He has little chance of getting on top of the job and clearing his desk and his mind for a month or two in order to take a long hard look at the future.

I once asked a priest from an Oxford college what he would do if he were Archbishop of Canterbury, and he said first of all he would summon all the bishops to Lambeth and tell them to stop doing whatever it was they were doing, and then he would give the whole Church a year's sabbatical. To this admirable plan I would add the suggestion that a secretariat should be left in charge, with the task of evaluating future strategy, and particularly with the task of re-organising the administrative machine. For a man who is a diocesan bishop (a full-time job in itself), a Metropolitan, president of the Lambeth Conference, a member of the Privy Council and the House of Lords, and with world-wide ecumenical interests, books to write and lectures to give and English dioceses and schools and universities to visit, the administrative machine that keeps his time-table intact and his mind on major issues can only, with the best will in the world, be described as a shambles. How else was it possible, for example, that on the Archbishop's return from a committee meeting of the World Council of Churches in Geneva in 1967 I could mention to him in the VIP lounge at Heathrow that I felt certain there would be considerable press interest in his views on the publication of the Commonwealth Immigrants Bill, particularly as he was then chairman of the National Committee for Commonwealth Immigrants, and that his household could blithely arrange for him to call on the Home Secretary to discuss the Bill without informing me? That weekend I took some eighty telephone calls.

No day in the life of Dr. Ramsey is entirely typical, but a random selection of engagements from his diary for the second fortnight in April, 1970 will give an indication of the breadth of his activities and the speed with which he is compelled to switch his mind from one subject to another. On the 15th he had engagements in his diocese. On the 16th he attended a board meeting of the Church Commissioners, and was back in Canterbury in the evening for a dinner with the European Conference of Churches. He remained in his diocese, fulfilling various engagements, for the next three days, and spent another three days, from the 20th to the 22nd, at a residential meeting of the British Council of Churches. On the 23rd he celebrated and preached in a London church, and gave a recorded television interview for the USA. On the 24th he attended the Standing Committee of Church Assembly, and was back in his diocese on the 25th, where he chaired a meeting at Christ Church College, Canterbury. He undertook further diocesan engagements on the 26th. On the 28th he conferred an honorary M.A. in the chapel at Lambeth Palace and on the 29th he was guest of honour at a meeting in a Hindu Temple in Golders Green.

This itinerary only forms an outline of the Archbishop's engagements for that period. It takes no account of the interviews he will have given, the letters he will have dictated, the sermons and talks he will have prepared, and the books he will have read late at night. There is a basic framework to Dr. Ramsey's day, which begins with Mattins in the chapel, followed by Holy Communion. At breakfast he reads the newspapers and his letters, and fairly speedily departs for his study. The schedule for each morning and afternoon varies according to the engagements in his diary; if the Archbishop and Mrs. Ramsey are at home without guests they lunch quite simply, serving themselves from a hot-plate at the sideboard. The Archbishop will have a glass of sherry before lunch, but there is usually only wine with the meal when they have guests. Mrs. Ramsey drinks very little; the Archbishop does not drink spirits or liqueurs, but enjoys sherry and wine and sometimes a glass of port. His tastes in food are essentially unsophisticated; he hates puddings of any kind, and his ideal meal would probably be soup or melon or grapefruit, a meat casserole and fruit and cheese. As soon as he has had a cup of coffee in the drawing-room the Archbishop is off again to his study. The household attend Evensong in the chapel, and the Archbishop and Mrs. Ramsey dine at seven. The ritual after dinner is the same as after lunch; one cup of coffee and straight back to the study.

The see of Canterbury has been occupied by 99 archbishops before Michael Ramsey. The spelling of its name has varied almost as much as the character of its occupants. Writing as late as 1719, to the Ambassador to the United Provinces, in connection with the death of Queen Anne, John Chamberlain referred to the Archbishop of Caunterburie. Few archbishops of Caunterburie can have had so auspicious a start to life in view of the major concern of their time as Dr. Ramsey, who was destined to become an international leader of the ecumenical movement; his father was a leading Congregationalist layman and his paternal grandfather was a Congregationalist minister, while his mother was an Anglican and her father was an Anglican priest. Perhaps in subconscious rebellion against his father's somewhat puritanical life, Dr. Ramsey embraced Anglicanism, and veered in his youth to the Anglo-Catholic wing of the Church of England. His personal churchmanship has remained catholic; but like most diocesan bishops, he has mellowed in public, and he is perfectly capable of being all things to all men. His public experience of ecumenism has in fact affected his personal appreciation of other people's attitudes and behaviour to quite a remarkable degree. He is now genuinely as happy sitting quietly at a Quaker prayer meeting as he is taking off and putting on his mitre as to the manner born during the Divine Liturgy in an Orthodox cathedral.

Michael Ramsey, one-hundredth Archbishop of Canterbury, Primate of All England and Metropolitan, was born on 14th November, 1904. He was educated at Repton and Magdalen College, Cambridge, where he was president of the Union and took a Second in the Classical Tripos and a First in Theology. He studied for the priesthood at Cuddesdon, and was ordained deacon in 1928 and priest a year later. He served as a curate of Liverpool parish church for three years, and from 1930-36 he was sub-warden of Lincoln Theological College. He then became Lecturer at Boston parish church, and for a year he was vicar of St. Benedict's, Cambridge. From 1940-50 Dr. Ramsey was Professor of Divinity at Durham University, and for the next two years he was Regius Professor of Divinity at Cambridge. In 1952 he was consecrated bishop of Durham. Four years later he was translated to the archbishopric of York, and in 1961, having failed to be consulted about the appointment of Dr. Fisher's successor he was not entirely surprised when a letter arrived inviting him to pack his bags once again and go to Canterbury.

It is said that President Truman was the only person who had no doubt that he would be elected President, and while ecclesiastical speculation ran fairly riot after Dr. Fisher had announced his intention to retire, I suspect that Dr. Ramsey was the only person who was certain he would succeed, and not just because Downing Street had not been canvassing his views on the man most suitable to become Primate of All England. The Archbishop has a shrewd assessment of his own capabilities, almost bordering on intellectual arrogance; he certainly regards himself as the most competent bishop on the bench. It is true there is not much competition at present, for the average intellectual standing of the bishops has probably never been lower. Dr. Ramsey tends to rate intellectual ability as the highest attribute a man can have, and he is not above expressing contempt for the speeches and actions of some of his brother bishops. His feelings of superiority never topple over into ill-manners, however; the worst thing he will ever say of someone is that he's an awful ass. The only man he has ever revered is William Temple.

It is because Dr. Ramsey sets so much store by intellectual

30

ability that he fights shy of men who act spontaneously, thinking with their hearts rather than their heads. For this reason he would rather see a suffragan-bishop of 62, whom he regards as "very able", which means he is good at steering legislation through the General Synod, go to the crucial see of Birmingham, rather than a younger man who might have some truly prophetic insights into the apparently intractable problem of making the gospel relative and attractive to an industrial society. The former bishop of Birmingham, the late Dr. Leonard Wilson, had the vision to appoint a chaplain to overseas people. It must have been obvious that by about 1969 the bishop would be retiring, but instead of earmarking the chaplain, Paul Burrough, for the diocese, in 1968 the Church of England let him slip through their fingers to become bishop of Mashonaland in Rhodesia.

Every Archbishop of Canterbury should be expected to have a basic programme, but he should be able to adapt himself to meet the particular needs of the Church as they arise while he is at Canterbury; but probably the most important single task to which any archbishop can address himself is the setting up of a strong bench of bishops. Here I would say the present Archbishop has failed to exercise his powers of patronage to a fairly serious extent. Indeed, his general interest in patronage is minimal. His former secretary, Mr. Robert Beloe, would have made a superb life peer, and although the suggestion was actually put to the Archbishop, he did nothing about it. He once told a priest who had resigned as secretary of one of the Councils of Church Assembly before being assured of another job — because he felt it right to make way for a new man — that he should live by faith. It was advice the man's wife no doubt found comforting when paying the grocery bills! This priest remained out of work for months, and is now largely wasted in a rural parish because the Archbishop would not encourage even a dean to make use of his special gifts.

It may be said in the Archbishop's defence that it is not his job to tell deans and other diocesan bishops whom to employ in their cathedrals and dioceses. According to the letter of the law, this is true. But Dr. Ramsey leans over too far backwards not to exercise his personal influence in the matter of appointments and employment generally, and he uses very little imagination in the bestowal of Lambeth degrees. He feels it wrong that he should seek secular preferment for members of his household, but in the case of Mr.

31

Beloe, whose gifts would have been placed at the service of the nation if the Archbishop had picked up the telephone and asked Mr. Wilson to give him a life peerage, I feel that he does not sufficiently appreciate that in an age when the State needs less and less the co-operation and approval of the Church the Archbishop has an increasing responsibility to exercise personal patronage when the nation stands to benefit.

When it comes to employment within the Church, Dr. Ramsey has personally never known financial worry since the age of 24, and he has an unworldly attitude towards other people's financial problems which borders on the insensitive. He also seems unable to grasp that the Church of England is big enough and secure enough to carry one or two leaders whose views on Christianity and society do not necessarily tally with his own. While enjoying a reputation for radicalism, the Archbishop is only really in favour of the implementation of radical ideas that alter the structure of Church life internally; he approves of most modern liturgical reform, and he would like to see a measure of disestablishment. But the secular implementation of the gospel in radical terms is not really for him, and he feels suspicious of anyone who might tend to rock the boat, even though to most observers it is perfectly obvious that the boat is already sinking!

For this reason the Archbishop is believed to have blocked the appointment to an English diocese of the Bishop of Cariboo, Dr. Ralph Dean, who had been seconded from his tiny Canadian diocese for five years to be executive officer of the Anglican Communion. At the end of that five year period, during which he acted with great distinction as episcopal secretary of the 1968 Lambeth Conference, Dr. Dean, an Englishman by birth, was the most knowledgeable leader anywhere in the world on matters concerning the Anglican Communion. He had travelled round the world five times, and he could have brought to the English Church first-hand knowledge of life as it is daily experienced by millions of less privileged Christians, and others, throughout the world. In other words, he could have brought to the Church of England a missionary zeal it so desperately needs; he could have destroyed some of our crippling parochialism. But the Archbishop is said not to have trusted him because he knew he tended to speak from his heart, and so back to Cariboo went Dr. Dean, and the Church of England lost a priceless opportunity of widening its own horizons.

Given freedom of choice in the part he plays in governing the Church of England, the Archbishop would personally have revelled in a system whereby the Primate was not automatically translated to a particular diocese. He has a passion for the north of England, and he would have been far happier as Archbishop of Durham than as Archbishop of Canterbury. His recollection of people and events concerned with his four years at Durham is prodigious, and he has a great affection for ugly northern towns and friendly northern people.

Given choice of freedom in his daily activities, Dr. Ramsey would opt for writing and reading, with some teaching contact with young men thrown in. Emotionally he feels threatened by men of his own generation; in ordinands especially he sees the seeds of the future Church, and to them he is emotionally drawn on religious grounds. Towards young men generally he shows a spontaneous affection and ease of manner often noticeably lacking towards other people he has to meet, and this can probably be accounted for by the natural paternal instincts any young man who might have been his son tends to draw out in him. When writing he becomes very excited by his own progress, and he has the ability to write fast and to snatch free moments without waiting for the inspired moment. He is in fact seldom happier than when he is working on a book. Last on his list of personal preferences comes the endless meetings, either pastoral or administrative, that clog his diary and over which he will fret and worry with the sort of sense of doom which a schoolboy will experience while waiting outside the headmaster's study.

In his contacts with people the Archbishop sometimes surprises himself, by fearing an encounter beforehand and then having to admit that he really rather enjoyed it. The well-known American singing group, The Temptations, once asked if the Archbishop would receive them as they wished to tell him about the work they were doing for community relations at home. They also admired the Archbishop's stand in this country on racial matters. I advised the Archbishop to find time to meet them, and he agreed to do so, saying he could only spare 20 minutes; after that he would be bored! In fact he spent 40 minutes with them, brushing aside their flattering remarks about his own attitudes to racialism, and questioning them closely on the American situation, with particular reference to the effect that the death of Martin Luther King had had. At the end of the interview, these highly professional entertainers, having received the Archbishop's blessing, went away completely captivated by him.

At practically every point the Archbishop's character contradicts itself. He can be a very wise person and academically has a brilliant mind, but he is liable to shift his ground ever so slightly in the interests of intellectual honesty and in so doing fails to give the clear-cut leadership that people naturally demand. But unlike the wisest men he will not often employ or seek the advice of people whose skills he does not himself possess, and he almost revels in a degree of laziness over matters which bore him. While undoubtedly he has got the ability to capitalise on a particular situation like his meeting with The Temptations, he all too seldom has the initiative to initiate such pastoral action himself. In Jamaica, for example, a police motor cyclist escorting his car crashed while swerving to avoid a lorry, and the policeman was rushed to hospital. As soon as we arrived at a boys' school, which happened to be the Archbishop's next engagement, where he was due to speak, I found a doctor, discovered which hospital the policeman had been taken to, found out there was just enough time to visit the hospital on the way to catch our airplane, and then sent up a note to the Archbishop asking if he would wish to go to the hospital. He read my note and gave me a nod.

When we arrived at the hospital the Archbishop held the man's hand, gave him a photograph, prayed with him and gave him his blessing. His action in going straight to the hospital was reported on the wireless and in the newspapers, and of course did much to enhance his reputation in Jamaica. The sad thing is that when the suggestion was put to him he was able to move into the pastoral situation so well, but without the suggestion being put to him in the first place he would never have gone to the hospital himself.

I think the reason for this is that his mind does not work fast in a crisis. But given time in which to think about a problem he does sometimes act with pastoral sympathy on his own initiative. A Fleet Street journalist was once in trouble with his editor over a bad error he had made in a story on the Archbishop. In the normal way I would have asked for a correction, but the journalist was still on trial on the newspaper, and seemed in fear of losing his job. I explained the situation to the Archbishop and said I hoped he would agree that I should let the matter slide. Not only did the Archbishop approve of this action but entirely on his own initiative

34

he also wrote a personal letter in his own hand to the journalist, telling him not to worry.

Side by side with the Archbishop's intellectual arrogance goes a genuine humility. He likes to be called Father by his household and Archbishop in public rather than Your Grace. When his official Daimler was due for replacement he insisted on a Ford, costing £1,000 less, not just to save money but because he really felt the Daimler was too grand. He would like Lambeth Palace to be renamed Lambeth House, and indeed I cannot quite see why he does not get his own way; if I were Archbishop of Canterbury and I wanted to change the name of Lambeth Palace to Lambeth House I would simply send a memo across the river to the Church Commissioners, and that would be an end of the matter! When he retires I doubt very much whether he will accept a peerage, and unlike Dr. Fisher, who asked that people should continue to address him as though he were still an archbishop, I believe Dr. Ramsey will merely wish to revert to the style and dignity of a retired bishop.

The Archbishop is essentially a lonely and sad man with no close friends apart from his wife and no one near him now who knows how to make him laugh, yet he has the most infectious sense of humour of any man I have ever known. Sometimes he will elaborate a situation into a story which he makes up under somewhat unexpected circumstances. Once, at a luncheon party at the Old Palace in Canterbury attended by an eminent patriach of the Orthodox Church, I jokingly remarked to the Archbishop that I rather fancied the see of St. Alban's, which at that time was vacant. He asked why, and I said I was particularly attached to the Abbey! Instantly the Archbishop began to compose a letter to the Prime Minister. "Dear Mr. Wilson," he dictated to the astonished guests, "I am writing to you about the bishopric of St. Alban's. You may think my request a little unusual, but I should be grateful if you would give your serious consideration to the appointment of my press officer, Mr. Michael De-la-Noy. . . . . " Heaven knows what stories circulate now behind the iron curtain about the way in which bishoprics are filled in the Church of England!

But even Dr. Ramsey's sense of humour can prove an embarrassment to him. I have known him start laughing at some thought or remark, and then begin to laugh almost uncontrollably, and then suddenly to stop and swing away as though he had been caught doing something unworthy. He is a man who bottles up his frustrations and impatience, so that he tends to walk very fast when he is worried about something, and to swish around on his toes, sometimes almost losing his balance as he does so.

His eccentricity is legendary, and with good reason. Not only would Dr. Ramsey be congenitally incapable of mending a fuse, he is the only man I know who can be relied on not even to know where to find the light switch. His touch in general with the mechanical world is non-existent. If he can walk into a door rather than through one he will. He is alarmingly accident-prone. In Puerto Rico he once stayed at the Bishop's house, which has a verandah outside the sitting room, which looks on to the sea through an entire wall of windows; in the middle of the windows is a glass door. Just before breakfast one morning, the Archbishop announced that he was going to inspect the view, and walked smack into a pane of glass, hitting his head quiet hard. That evening, just before a supper party, he repeated his desire to inspect the view, got up and walked smack into the same pane of glass. On departing from the house the next morning for the airport the Archbishop said goodbye to all the staff and relations, stepped backwards over a ledge not more than three inches high, and toppled over backwards on to a concrete path, folding up as he did so like a porcupine. Mrs. Ramsey, the chaplain and I stood paralysed for a second; I had visions of remaining in Puerto Rico for some weeks and was already mentally drafting a message to PA. However, when we helped the Archbishop to his feet he was completely unharmed and, unlike the rest of us, apparently unalarmed.

A few moments later I was nearly run over by the Archbishop's car, and we were all hoping the third accident would happen before the airplane took off. Fortunately it occurred shortly after we were airborne, when Mrs. Ramsey managed to send a tray of coffee and drinks flying all over herself and the Archbishop. The Archbishop is very brave when he does suffer physical pain. In Trinidad he was quite badly hurt when the driver started up the car after he had stopped it outside the Bishop's house, and the Archbishop was already getting out. His leg was badly grazed and must have been very painful. I bathed it for him and got him a drink while Mrs. Ramsey was making plans to cancel the dinner engagement that night. But the Archbishop soon recovered, and insisted on running up the stairs two steps at a time to prove that he was well enough to go out.

The Archbishop's eccentricity is often manifest in a charming but sometimes also rather dangerous unworldliness. It is dangerous when it takes no account of life as most people understand it and have to live it. It can be dangerous too when he is faced with a plate of prawns, and attacks them with a knife and fork, carving them in half and eating them, shells and all. It can be expensive when he buys a 300 year old house for his retirement without having it surveyed, only to discover dry rot in the one beam holding up the dining-room ceiling. It can be disconcerting when he drives through a town, muttering the name of the town twenty or thirty times to himself. It can be hurtful when the eccentricity mingles with egocentricity, and he will walk away while someone is telling him a story, or go on signing letters while giving an interview. It can be touchingly funny when he tries to uncork a bottle of wine, with singularly small success, but still insists, after someone has helped to get the cork out, that he should pour out the wine.

Because of a strong streak of egocentricity in his nature the Archbishop is happiest when he is the centre of attention, or else when he is completely alone. He is always ill at ease in a crowded room. But if he meets someone with whom he has a rapport, and with whom he begins to have a conversation on a subject he cares deeply about, he can then cut off entirely from everybody else in the room and become totally obsessed with the matter currently on his mind. It is common knowledge that he has no small talk, and he simply will not do anything to cultivate any. He is uncompromising in his relations with people; he will do nothing to get on to your wavelength. Either you get on to his or you never meet. He is at his most brilliant in small groups when he is talking on subjects that interest him and he has intelligent people questioning him. He is an erratic public speaker, but he has the gift of thinking on his feet, and he always makes extremely good impromptu after-dinner speeches. The public engagements he most dreads are the speeches he has to make in the House of Lords, and while waiting to make his own speech he is in fact in a state of complete nerves.

The Archbishop cannot bear to be under attack. He feels too easily threatened by letters criticising some action he has taken, or by people whose views he feels tiresome but who have to be met and listened to. Above all, he is sensitive to the printed word. He is generally the first to spot a newspaper article about himself and to have read it before anyone else. If it is flattering, he will draw people's attention to it. If it is critical, he will let it prey on his mind, instead of remembering that tomorrow's fish will probably be sold in it.

There has been a long tradition of wrapping the Archbishop in cotton-wool, of protecting him from the realities of life and the true nature of the world instead of exposing him to them. Had he remained a don this would not have mattered. I think that for an archbishop he is too protected for his own good and for the good of the Church, for while he experiences acutely causes and ideas, he has no real emotional understanding of the intellectual concepts he champions.

And by long undisciplined habit the Archbishop often feels free to hide behind his eccentricity, using it as an excuse to avoid duties that he does not wish to perform or contacts with people he wishes to avoid. By nature he is not a good administrator, but so chaotic is the administration of his household that a proper sense of responsibility would have prompted him long ago to call in professional administrative assistance, and to hand over to others the tasks he personally finds so uncongenial. Simply the way in which the daily correspondence is dealt with is hair-raising. One of the porters will bring the basket of letters into the breakfast room, all neatly laid out. He hands Mrs. Ramsey's letters to her, the chaplain's letters to him, and then places the basket in front of the Archbishop. From that moment all conversation ceases. The Archbishop descends on the letters as a schoolboy might descend on a pile of doughnuts. He looks at the envelopes that seem interesting, tossing the others on one side. Some he opens, some he drops on the floor; others get marmalade spread on them, some get passed to Mrs. Ramsey to read. Then suddenly the Archbishop will scoop up the letters and disappear to the study. Some letters may get answered that day; some may get torn up if the Archbishop feels threatened by their contents. They may get passed to a secretary or chaplain. They may get stuffed into his cassock and forgotten.

When the Archbishop gets a subject on his mind he can become absolutely obsessed by it, sometimes with amusing, if genuinely eccentric, results. At the time of the Leasco take-over of Pergamon Press the Archbishop suddenly developed a keen interest in Mr. Robert Maxwell and his business interests. A photographer was due from an agency to take some pictures of the Archbishop, and as I was trying to show the photographer and his assistant out of the study the Archbishop kept calling me back, apparently in some agitation. I closed the door and, sounding very excited, the Archbishop asked, "Were they Maxwell's lot?"

Politically, the Archbishop is two different people as well. In many ways he has an astute sense of political timing and of what it is best to say and do, and when and where. In other ways he can misjudge an atmosphere disastrously, or fail to seize the initiative when a marvellous opportunity presents itself of gaining a platform for his views. But when it is pointed out to him that he has misjudged a situation he is nearly always quick to put the matter right, if it is possible to do so. The World Council of Churches once asked him to chair a session at a Conference on race relations in Notting Hill. The Archbishop treated the occasion as though he were in the chair at Church Assembly, surrounded by people who played cricket and understood standing orders. Mr. Shar, a leader in this country of the Black Power movement, wished to speak, and although strictly he was out of order, it was obvious the conference wanted to hear him, but the Archbishop refused to let him speak. Mr. Shar promptly left the room and gave an interview to the press. When the Archbishop's secretary sent a note up to him saying that he and I both felt that he had misjudged the wishes of the conference, and suggesting that he might like to express regret, back came the note with the single word "Yes" written in a circle. When the session ended, the Archbishop said he was sorry if he had offended the conference or Mr. Shar, and as the press filed out a reporter from the *Daily Express* just said to me, "Very handsome!"

The Archbishop was once booked to speak on "Christianity and Freedom" at the London School of Economics at a time when the LSE and students generally were very much in the news. Every newspaper and television station sent a reporter, and the Archbishop could have used the opportunity to get the headlines on any subject of his choosing. But he insisted on sticking to his brief, with the kind of stubbornness that goes well in company with some great moral issue but was hardly appropriate on this occasion. He succeeded in boring stiff the audience and the press for forty of the most embarrassing minutes I have ever lived through, and not a single word of what he said was reported the next day. In terms of seizing the advantage of a ready-made platform the engagement was a complete fiasco.

The Archbishop needs his morale boosting; he needs encouraging when he has done well and cheering up when he has failed. But his staff sometimes find this too much of a one-sided operation. The Archbishop's agonising shyness, which is really a flight from life, too often prevents him from expressing heartfelt sympathy or heartfelt happiness towards others, and it is an almost total barrier to physical contact. He cannot really bear people to be ill, for this makes demands upon his patience that he finds a bore, and if someone personally known to him undergoes a bereavement or some other tragedy he finds it almost impossible to make more than a perfunctory remark of condolence. Essentially the Archbishop deals in abstracts; he will pursue an idea to the ends of the earth but he will undertake very little in the way of actual deeds for individual human beings. And his judgments of people are incredibly erratic, because all his judgments tend to be clouded by irrational prejudices. But despite all these considerable drawbacks in one charged to be a pastor and a Father-in-God, the Archbishop does enjoy great love and loyalty from his staff. He can become very depressed but he has very quick powers of recovery, and although too often he becomes visibly bored during a public engagement he has got a lively ability to greet people with infectious joy whenever he enters a room or gets out of his car.

One of the most fascinating aspects of the Archbishop's life is that in effect he is condemned to undergo a morganatic marriage; while his own position in society is regulated by the order of precedence, which places him immediately after the Royal Family, and his position in the Church is unparalleled outside the College of Cardinals, his wife shares in none of the secular or ecclesiastical honours. The Archbishop always walks in front of Mrs. Ramsey; he gets out of the car before her and he is received before her, and there are certain functions he even attends without her. His absent mindedness is not beyond enabling him to wander off without waiting to see that she is safely following. The story has been told by Wilfred De'Ath of the day in Guyana when Mrs. Ramsey accidentally found herself walking in front of the Archbishop, and stepping aside said, "Sorry darling, I didn't mean to walk in front of you." Mrs. Ramsey is probably more conscious of the Archbishop's role and persona than he is, although on State occasions he does move and behave with inherent dignity,

On September 24, 1969, the Archbishop celebrated the 40th anniversary of his ordination to the priesthood with a Sung Eucharist in Westminster Abbey. Earlier in the afternoon he and Mrs. Ramsey met photographers in the garden at Lambeth Palace, and entertained a group of journalists to tea.

Photograph by UPI

The Archbishop is caught by Jane Bown of *The Observer* in a typical pose as he listens to Mrs. Martin Luther King speaking at a luncheon in London given to mark the publication of her autobiography.

sometimes humming hymn tunes to himself while walking in procession! He has a disconcerting habit of rocking backwards and forwards fairly forcefully on his heels if he has to stand still for any length of time. But in cope and mitre he looks magnificently mediaeval, floating metaphorically above the earthly scene over which he happens to be presiding.

The Archbishop's lack of pomposity and awareness of his own inherent importance was apparent one day when he attended a private luncheon at a newspaper office. No one was present to receive him on his arrival. When eventually he was shown upstairs to the dining-room, where drinks were being served before lunch, the members of the staff invited to lunch with him all arrived after the Archbishop. I thought the arrangements a disgraceful shambles, but I am certain the Archbishop had no idea they were. Once the conversation had gripped him he was able to go away having genuinely enjoyed himself, regarding the occasion as a great success, as indeed in the long-run of course it was.

With Mrs. Ramsey the Archbishop shares a remarkable memory for people and places overseas. He can reel off the names and dioceses of overseas bishops, he retains an almost infallible memory for places he has visited on overseas tours, and his store of anecdotes about things that have amused him or things that have proved a particularly memorable bore is always well stocked. He loves travelling overseas, for then he feels free from the emotional and physical demands made upon him by the crowding in of events and engagements at home which he does not much enjoy. In his heart, he despairs of the Church of England's ability to excite him, just as the Church of England despairs of his ability to wave a magic wand and make all manner of things well.

At home, the Archbishop is very much a prophet in his own land. Overseas, he is readily treated, by complete strangers, as a priest. In New York, a coloured press photographer, denied admittance to a private lecture, was not in the least concerned about missing his photograph but asked whether the Archbishop would give him his blessing. As soon as Dr. Ramsey stepped from the rostrum, having covered himself in glory by delivering a stunning dissertation to 300 awe-struck bishops of the Episcopal Church in the U.S.A., I introduced him to the photographer, and instantly Dr. Ramsey became totally unaware of his surroundings, intent only upon the man and his own priestly function.

Again, after a particularly tiring day in New York, when the Archbishop had disrobed after a service late at night, a young woman went up to him in the vestry and asked if he would bless her crucifix. Without a moment's hesitation Dr. Ramsey again became totally absorbed in the woman and the prayers he was saying to her. She stepped back and exclaimed, "Truly, you are a child of God!" I have yet to hear anyone in England, in public, react to the Archbishop's priestly office in such an uninhibited way. In countries like Nigeria and Trinidad, children have been known to walk fifty miles just to see him pass.

The Archbishop can be moved by scenery, but he has no other very highly-developed aesthetic sense; his interest in music extends no further than Church music and Gilbert and Sullivan, and he reads practically nothing but theology and political biography. At his own intellectual level he writes extremely well but he has no popular touch, and while he finds it easy to talk to students he has no contact worth talking about with little children. He never goes to the theatre or the cinema, he never watches television or listens to the wireless, he hardly ever dines out except when invited officially, and he and Mrs. Ramsey entertain privately at home very little indeed. His whole life revolves around his religion; he is fascinated by Christianity and theology, but the world God actually made is for him in far too many ways a closed and indeed unread book.

CHAPTER THREE

THE CHURCH
AND ITS PUBLIC IMAGE

There is only one thing in the world worse than being talked about, and that is not being talked about: Oscar Wilde.

ANY office charged with the job of creating or presenting an image of a larger organisation will in the process create an image of itself, and this image will reflect on its client. It is true that total control of the Church of England's reputation will always remain beyond the grasp of the Church Information Office, for any curate is perfectly capable of leaping on to the front pages by baking a cake in the pulpit without consulting the C.I.O. first, but nevertheless the image of the Church of England will always depend to a large extent on the competence of the staff of the C.I.O., and particularly upon the degree of professionalism they display in their dealings with the press.

The Church of England is not a product that needs to be sold, like Macleans toothpaste; by virtue of its historical position in society and the continuing interest shown by sceptics and believers alike in the spiritual wares it peddles the Church is likely to retain for some time a potentially enormous share of newsprint and radio and television time without any direct expenditure of money. But because the Church of England is part of the national establishment it is peculiarly vulnerable to attack if it makes a fool of itself, and because its senior hierarchy take their place beside the other rulers of the nation they are automatically liable to fall hard if they fall at all.

So in terms of public relations the Church of England requires an organisation capable of interpreting the antique vagaries of the

Church to a secularist society, capable of explaining, too, the continuing relevance of its beliefs, worship and witness, and capable of encouraging an understanding of the imprecise balance between orthodoxy and modernism that so maddeningly but fascinatingly distinguishes a Church that claims to be both catholic and reformed. Above all, it requires an organisation able to recognise that inevitably there will be a focusing of interest on personalities — particularly on the personality of the Archbishop of Canterbury — while encouraging a broad acceptance of the Church as an imperfect but credible body of men and women who collectively believe in a gospel of love and who care more for society than for themselves.

It is the Church Information Office, one of the boards and councils of the General Synod listed in Chapter One, whose delicate task it is to build a bridge between St. Augustine and Sir Max Aitken. The C.I.O. first came into prominence under Colonel Robert Hornby, its first Chief Information Officer, who between 1960-65 built up its reputation as a P.R. outfit prepared to compete in Fleet Street on an equal footing with any secular organisation. For this he gained respect. As a journalist myself while Robert Hornby was in charge of the C.I.O., I certainly recall being impressed by the way he ran press conferences and disseminated news. If Colonel Hornby tended to veer slightly towards the hearty he was always accessible, he was not afraid to talk off the record, and he appreciated the vital premise that all good public relations stem from good personal relations.

When Colonel Hornby resigned he was succeeded by Major-General Adam Block. General Block was fifty-seven. At the age of twenty he had been commissioned in the Royal Artillery, and it was as a regular soldier that he experienced life for the next thirty-four years. In the last year of the war he was awarded the D.S.O. His peace-time promotion from major to major-general was fairly routine. In 1959 he was appointed G.O.C., Malta, and he retired from the active list in 1962 with a C.B. and a C.B.E.

The General did not used to be ashamed to advertise his recreations in *Who's Who* as shooting, fishing, riding, golf and tennis, although now they merely constitute 'all country pursuits', and one would have thought that a contented country life awaited him at his Hampshire home upon his retirement. However, he did not marry until he was thirty-seven, and it may have been the prospect of having to educate three daughters on half-pay that prompted him to take a civilian job. He became personal assistant to the chairman of David Brown. The General's appeal to the Church Information Advisory Committee, who appointed him Chief Information Officer in 1965 on a five-year contract, was perhaps that by temperament he was unlikely to rock the boat, that he possessed a quiet and rather charming personality, and above all that with his military background (his father and his father-in-law were colonels and his brother is a brigadier), with his own rank of major-general and his decorations he was nothing if not respectable.

But the General had only been in Church House a week when the first broadside was fired, from the correspondence columns of the *Church Times*. "No doubt," wrote the Reverend Norman Hood, " 'Praise the Lord and pass the ammunition' is as good a motto as any for Church House, and this may explain why a major-general succeeds a full colonel as Chief Information Officer. But why stop at major-general? There are several field-marshals unemployed."

Mr. Hood went on to ask whether those responsible for making the appointment imagined that Fleet Street was destitute of a top-ranking journalist or public relations expert commanding wide contacts in Fleet Street and in radio and television. "There is a wealth of goodwill for the Church in the press and other channels of mass communication," he went on, "and it might be a good idea if this were drawn upon for membership of the committee controlling the Church House Information Office. I feel that very few of the present members know much about what should be their subject."

Another letter appeared in the same issue, from the Reverend Eric Thomas, who said he failed to understand what a man who had spent his entire adult life in the army could possibly offer God through this appointment. His criticism, he said, was directed at those responsible for making the appointment.

"After thirty-four years in the strange, directed life of officers' mess, Staff College and High Command," wrote Mr. Thomas, "where 'Sir' is a compulsory address (not necessarily one of respect), and where 'jump to it!' is the order of the day (and every day), General Block, the distinguished soldier, is now responsible for the public image of the Church in this country . . . . . He must now direct or project the Church to people whose civilian way of life cannot be known, and one, when it becomes known to him, he will not be able to understand. I regret to say that I think this could be just another step in the alienating of the Church from the majority of the people."

A week later, in a pen-portrait, the *Church Times* did its best to balance these letters with a piece which described the General as a quiet, modest man, which indeed he is. But the battle was not over. On July 9th, the *Church Times* reported, "General's Appointment Comes Under Fire in Church Assembly."

During a debate on the annual report of the Standing Committee of the C.I.O. on July 5th, some seven weeks after the General had taken up his appointment, the Reverend Adrian Esdaile, a member for Southwark, attacked the committee responsible for appointing General Block, and reminded the Assembly that the advertisement the General had answered had said that the applicant should have experience of public relations, be conversant with the requirements of the press, and have wide contacts with the press, radio and television. He asked whether the image of a retired major-general whose hobbies appeared to be fly-fishing and fox-hunting gave the right impression to journalists or to people in the parishes.

There are said to have been thirty applicants for the job. Replying to Mr. Esdaile, the Bishop of London, who had chaired the committee that made the appointment, said that they had had to steer a course between the techniques of the public relations officer whose duty was to answer complaints or to sell something to the public which might be slightly resistant to receiving it, and on the other hand having someone who was experienced in the techniques of publicity and particularly of journalism. The committee had interviewed applicants of varying experience who tended to go to one or the other side of the two fields. They had not found anyone who in their judgment had the personality and the breadth of vision to hold the two in balance. General Block had the vision and experience that they were looking for, the ability to make his contacts where he did not already possess them, and, above all, the capacity to work with and build up a staff who would give the C.I.O. the continuity that it needed.

The Bishop ended this rather novel and to my mind extremely muddled defence of his own unique understanding of the qualifications needed in a chief information officer with an attack on an interview with the General that had appeared in *The Evening News*, saying that it misrepresented statements made by the General, and was "a most irresponsible article which could not be condemned in too strong terms as inaccurate." One wonders, if the Bishop had not been present at the interview, how he knew that the statements made by the General had in fact been misrepresented. It was in any case an inauspicious start to the General's career as a press officer to have his first interview with a journalist corrected for him in public, by the man who had just appointed him.

My own first meeting with General Block took place when I was working as a journalist. I did not know him by sight, but discovered later that I had been sitting next to him at a press conference at Church House. The conference was to launch an appeal for money to build an Orthodox church in Birmingham, and I was somewhat surprised, remembering how Robert Hornby used to run press conferences himself, to find Prince Tomislav of Yugoslavia in the chair on his own. At the end of the press conference General Block turned to me and said, "Jolly interesting questions, weren't they." I agreed, and repaired to the bar for a drink. A friend from the B.B.C. then introduced me to the General as he came up to join us, and I realised, with some astonishment, who he was.

My second encounter was at a party at Timothy Beaumont's house. By way of polite cocktail conversation I asked the General if he was enjoying his new job. He assured me that he was, even though at times he felt as though he were walking along a parapet, with some of the people firing up at him and some of them firing down . . . .

The General was of course meeting other journalists at this time. At a party in Fleet Street early one evening he was introduced to a couple of senior Fleet Street men, one the night news editor of *The Daily Telegraph*, the other an assistant editor on *The Times*. To the gentleman from *The Daily Telegraph* the General remarked that it must be nice for him now that his day's work was over and everything in his office was packing up. The first edition had not of course even gone to bed! In an effort to retrieve an embarrassing situation the assistant editor of *The Times* kindly offered to show General Block round the new *Times* building, then only recently opened. The General said that he would like this very much, as he had never been round a newspaper office before . . . .

General Block began his job at the C.I.O. with two fairly serious disadvantages; he knew nothing about the communications industry, and he knew nothing about the Church. On his own disarming admission to me, he once said, "When I first came here I didn't know the difference between a dean and an archdeacon." He was also very ready to admit that the press was not his strong point. More serious than the General's inability to distinguish between two gentlemen both in gaiters was his inability to understand the kind of political games that ecclesiastics get up to, and thus to be able to evaluate the things they were doing and saying. He likes to regard himself as the original man in the pew, the sensible, level-headed, rural churchgoer who knows nothing of high or low, and is neither radical nor conservative. At the rural parish level this may be very admirable, but it hardly helps one to understand and communicate what is going on in Church House, where the clashes between high and low, conservatives and radicals do still take place and do still affect many of the major decisions taken by the Church.

Over the years the General has of course picked up a basic working knowledge of ecclesiastical administration, but I doubt that he yet understands the nuances of Church life, and I am certain he does not understand the demands society makes on the Church today to justify its credibility. On the press side, journalists remain an enigma to him, and no doubt he to them, partly because he will keep serving them South African sherry. There is quite simply no natural affinity, and on the General's side a perfectly understandable inability to understand even the basic mechanics of the journalist's trade.

The office over which General Block presides has grown considerably in recent years, and its current budget exceeds £56,000. For the first two years he ran the press office with a staff of two, and employed a clergyman as radio and television officer. Despite advice to the effect that nowadays the dissemination of news to press, radio and television is regarded by most people in the business as part of one operation the General has always insisted on retaining two separate departments.

The largest department within the C.I.O. is the publishing division and the bookshop. There is also an enquiry centre. The total staff is around thirty.

Robert Hornby had looked after the Archbishop of Canterbury's press relations, and General Block continued to exercise this special brief. His relations with Dr. Ramsey were cordial, but never intimate. There was an amusing if slightly tense occasion on the

48

Archbishop's 1967 visit to the U.S.A. It had become obvious that the Archbishop would have to commit himself to a view on the Vietnam War, and after briefing himself before leaving for America the Archbishop decided to say that while he revered those who had given their lives in what they had regarded as a just cause he felt bound to say that the war was one which neither side could win, and that America should pull out. When the General began, on tour, to offer gratuitous military advice, the Archbishop told him he was not concerned with military strategy so much as ethics, and that if Adam didn't like publicising the line he had decided to take he could go and run the Boys Brigade!

The only time I have seen the Archbishop angry was after a dinner party at Lambeth Palace, when the guests had gone and the Archbishop was sitting on a sofa in the corridor, discussing with his domestic chaplain and myself arrangements for a new series of press lunches. It transpired that the General had blithely announced that he intended going to the lunches, when it had already been agreed that those present should consist only of the Archbishop, eight members of the press, a chaplain and myself. Even Mrs. Ramsey had foregone the pleasure of being hostess in her own home in order that the lunches should be put on a working basis.

"I don't want two people from the C.I.O.," the Archbishop said, stamping his heel on the floor. "I can't cope with two people from the C.I.O. Nobody comes here unless they are invited by me. I won't have it! I won't have it!"

Even when the General received a letter from the Archbishop telling him his desire was that only I should attend the lunches the General seemed oblivious of his tactless behaviour, rationalising the situation by saying that he did not mind who went to the lunches so long as he was kept informed which people were coming from the press. Every time there was a press lunch the General would laboriously write down each guest's name, most of whom were household names but of none of whom he seemed to have heard, and he would ask if I could arrange for him to meet the journalists afterwards. The incident of the press lunches illustrates in a relatively mild way the dilemma in which I was increasingly to find myself as I tried to serve two masters, the Archbishop and the General.

In 1966 the Archbishop paid a visit to Pope Paul. Robert Hornby was in Rome at the time, and although the General went with the

Archbishop, Robert Hornby was called in to lend a hand. The arrangement made perfectly sound sense in practical terms, but how any self-respecting professional man could enjoy having his immediate predecessor in tow during a major test of his own abilities I do not understand. Whatever General Block's private view of the matter may have been (and my guess is he was genuinely only too glad to have someone to look after him) he always said afterwards that it had been a sensible thing because "two heads are better than one."

Between the somewhat unusual visit to Rome and the American assignment the General was faced with a major crisis at home. This occurred over Rhodesia. The Archbishop was in the chair during a debate on Rhodesia on October 26th, 1965 at a meeting in Aberdeen of the British Council of Churches. The Archbishop decided to intervene in the debate in an effort to clarify the issues which he thought lay before the Council. He spoke without any previous intention to do so, and therefore without notes. The core of his speech was a slightly muddled plea for Christians to support armed intervention in Rhodesia in the event of the British Government deciding on such a course of action. The Archbishop said, "If the British Government thought it practicable to use force for the protection of the rights of the Rhodesian people then I think that as Christians we have to say that it would be right to use force to that end."

I say that the statement was slightly muddled because whether it would have been right to use force was surely the issue, not whether Christians should support the government if the government decided on a course of action which individual Christians might regard as immoral. In any event, the balloon went up. The press were almost universally hostile; Nicolas Stacey came to the Archbishop's rescue in *The Evening News* and Monica Furlong in the *Daily Mail*, but otherwise the newspapers reflected editorially and in their cartoons a vast measure of public outrage. There was talk of a motion of censure in the House of Commons, *The Times* letter columns nearly boiled over, and the Archbishop was generally depicted as both a warmonger and politically inept, for his speech was made while the Prime Minister, Mr. Wilson, was actually in Salisbury negotiating with Ian Smith.

Despite an item on the agenda about Rhodesia, coming as it did at such a critical time, it did not occur to General Block to accompany the Archbishop to Aberdeen, and the first he knew of the speech was when he heard a report of it on the wireless. The Archbishop took part that night in a radio interview, but no attempt was made to call a press conference in order for him to be questioned on his views and for the record to be put straight. The General's philosophy for disaster is always to believe that if you ignore something long enough it will go away. The taste of the Rhodesian speech has never gone away. The Archbishop believes in retrospect that he was naive to have spoken on the subject where he did and when he did, and he has described the press coverage and the avalanche of abusive letters he received as 'crucifying'. As soon as the dust had begun to settle the suggestion was planted in his ear that if he wanted to avoid any more unpleasant publicity, and more to the point if he wanted to have projected a positive impression of his views on matters of national and ecclesiastical importance, he would be well advised to hire a professional press officer. This view was strengthened in October 1966 when the Archbishop made some comments in Canada on the effectiveness of Billy Graham's crusades, and on his return he was defended in the press by his secretary instead of his chief information officer. Finally he had to write a letter himself to *The Times*.

As an exercise in public relations, it is only possible in all honesty to say that General Block's handling of the Rhodesia crisis was a disaster. But he should never have been expected to be able to handle such a situation, and what continued to amaze those members of Church Assembly who thought the Church Information Office should be helped back on to a respected footing was that the Church Information Advisory Committee should continue to believe that a retired major-general was the right sort of person to be in a post requiring flair, fast thinking, imagination and the ability to anticipate a course of events — and to act upon that anticipation — in a field as land-mined with its own disciplines as any military field of battle.

It was decided that the General was not to be criticised for his lack of expertise and that he was to retain his post as Chief Information Officer while relinquishing direct responsibility for the Archbishop. A professional press officer to the Archbishop was to be appointed, who would also be firmly rooted in the Church Information Office as assistant information officer. Responsibility for the Archbishop's public relations would however remain divided between his press officer and the C.I.O. radio and television officer. Into this administratively crazy set-up I blithely stepped on or around the Feast Day of St. Michael and All Angels, 1967.

In retrospect I can now see that the seeds of disaster had already been sown before my first interview, for obviously there had not been any clear consultation between the Archbishop and the Church Information Office. At my interview, Sir John Scott took the chair in the General's office; the General was present, together with Mr. Robert Beloe, at that time secretary to the Archbishop, Mr. Vaughan Reynolds, a former editor of *The Birmingham Post* and a member of the Church Information Advisory Committee, and the Reverend David Skinner, shortly to resign as radio and television officer.

I was told that Mr. Edgar Holt, chief press officer, was due to retire after the 1968 Lambeth Conference, and that it was considered advisable to recruit a replacement for him on the press side before the Conference actually took place, and that if I joined the C.I.O. I should also have something to do with the Archbishop, but my duties in this respect were left extremely vague.

The next day the General telephoned to say that the Archbishop wished to see me. As soon as I met the Archbishop in his study at Lambeth Palace it became apparent that his conception of my duties was radically different. He was quite specific in stating that he wished me to be his personal press officer, answerable to him as far as my work in connection with him was concerned. "They should have told you this," he kept saying to me, "they should have told you this."

The Archbishop's conception of the job certainly made it appear far more interesting than the Committee who had interviewed me had led me to believe would be the case. As I was obviously going to become closely identified with the Archbishop I felt it right to remind him that as a member of Church Assembly, from which I imagined I would have to resign, I was regarded as a radical, and that having been assistant editor of *Prism* I was suspect among the more conservative Church journalists. The Archbishop said this did not worry him at all, and told me, "If you become my press officer I shall be both personally and professionally delighted."

On the question of resigning from Church Assembly, and curtailing some of my freelance activities as a writer, the Archbishop jokingly remarked, "There will of course be sacrifices to be made,

52

but I imagine that one of the lesser sacrifices will be resigning from the House of Laity!" He made no specific request about not free-lancing, but merely indicated that presumably I should not feel free to write on controversial Church matters, a general principle with which I readily agreed.

Shortly after the interview with the Archbishop I was formally offered the job as his press officer, and General Block also created for me the new title of assistant information officer, thus placing me in the C.I.O. as his immediate second-in-command. At no time did the General or Sir John Scott discuss with me the question of freelance writing. My appointment was officially announced as the Archbishop was leaving for his summer holiday, and in his own hand he wrote a letter to me from the hotel in Devon where he was staying. In the light of future events the letter turns out to have contained a hope that has been tragically unfulfilled. "I am sure you will bring great help to me," the Archbishop wrote, "and I will try to be a good learner about when and where to drop my bricks!"

Planning for the Lambeth Conference was already under way when I joined the C.I.O. and one of the first tasks I was given was to edit a brochure called *Lambeth '68*. This contained a foreword by the Archbishop, and articles on the Anglican Communion and the history of the Lambeth Conference, together with details of the agenda and the names of the chairmen and secretaries of the various committees. As many of the 500 bishops due to attend, together with their wives and children, had never been to London before and would be in England for at least a month, I included some light-hearted hints on the British way of life, a list of places of interest to see, and a list of eight restaurants, varying in price from the very cheap to the relatively expensive.

In view of the poverty in which some of the bishops, particularly those from Africa and the Middle East, are accustomed to work, and the question of world poverty in general with which the Con-ference was due to concern itself, it was considered by some people that the inclusion of the list of restaurants was insensitive, a point of view I can certainly understand; and in view of the righteous indignation to which I should have realised the brochure would give rise I certainly believe now that to have published the list of restaurants was bad P.R. In defence, it was said by others that this particular entry was symptomatic of the tensions within Christianity, focused in the fact that plenty of wealthy American bishops would most certainly be eating out in the West End, and that it was hypocritical to pretend otherwise.

Whatever the wisdom of including restaurants in the brochure, the result was an early indication of the way future events might be handled. The Archbishop had no comment to make on the brochure until he began to receive a few private complaints. Then he said he wanted the offending page deleted in some way or other. I pointed out that the brochure was already printed and that to start re-designing it or obliterating an entry once it had been seen by the press would only cause additional publicity and comment. He accepted this advice, but said that if the brochure came under attack in the Conference he might have to denounce it. I asked him not to do anything so rash; everyone knew I had been the editor, and I should be asked what it felt like to be denounced in public by my boss. I pointed out that this could only result in embarrassment for both of us. The Archbishop saw the point, and kept quiet. Not so the Archbishop of York, who went on the wireless to call the brochure a major P.R. blunder. Sure enough, the next morning I was telephoned by *The Evening News*, who wanted to know what it felt like to be denounced in public by Dr. Coggan! For the first and last time in my three years as a press officer I gave that fatuous reply "no comment."

I can also see how, early on, in view of the Lambeth Conference, strained relations between the General and myself had their origin. Once the General has conceded a point relating to a short-term issue he relaxes about the matter, and harbours no resentment. But it is often difficult, and sometimes impossible, to convince him to change his mind where long-term planning is concerned. It was the opinion of the episcopal secretary of the Lambeth Conference that it would be administratively better for me to run the press conferences rather than the General, a view I felt bound to share. It was fairly easy to persuade the General that it would be proper for me to look after the opening and closing press conferences, as the Archbishop would be presiding at these, but it needed a firm request from the episcopal secretary that I should run the daily press briefings as well before this matter was properly resolved. While with part of his mind I am sure the General acquiesced with a good grace, with part of his mind I am equally sure he began to realise that many of his duties were about to be taken over by a

54

subordinate, and it cannot have been easy for a man in a senior position to have to acknowledge to himself that in a major sphere for which he was responsible he was just not regarded as professionally competent.

My personal relationship with General Block was built in the first place on a basis of mutual respect; I could not pretend to approve of his appointment as Chief Information Officer, but I liked him personally, and I certainly had no plans to engineer a coup! I tried to accept the rôle in which I had been placed as that of a loyal subordinate who was paid to advise a senior figurehead. But in the field of public relations it was not sufficient simply to offer General Block advice and do what I could to keep him away from journalists, thus keeping both him and the Church out of harm; events often moved too fast to allow me time to tell him everything I was doing, and before long I was taking executive decisions on my own initiative. The press soon got into the habit of telephoning me at home not just about matters directly related to the Archbishop but about a whole range of Church affairs, and most weekends I received ten or a dozen calls at home, while nearly every evening I dealt with one or two telephone enquiries, and if a big story broke I could be on the telephone all evening. The General gave few indications of resentment, but in the light of later developments I have to wonder whether a dangerous sense of inadequacy was not in fact building up.

There were other personnel problems in the office which should not have existed in a P.R. outfit emotionally equipped to project a public image of a client specializing in love. The General was, in my view, a very erratic judge of character, and at least two exceptionally talented young members of the staff, one in the publishing division and one in the press office, would never have been engaged unless in the early days I had had a sufficient measure of the General's confidence to be able to advise him to hire them. The length of a man's hair seemed to be the General's criteria for employment rather than a measure of flair and imagination. My own position with other members of the staff on the communications side was not helped by being the only professional; there is a strong tradition in the Church of anti-professionalism, and a strong bias in favour of the clergy, and I had to deal with a retired major-general and a former parish priest! My repeated pleas for a re-construction of the office in order to have one organisation for the dissemination of news to the press, radio and television, and to have overall responsibility for the Archbishop's public relations under one umbrella, went unheeded because they were met on emotional rather than professional grounds. I felt, rightly or wrongly, that General Block exercised too little pastoral responsibility for his staff, many of whom came to me rather than the General with personal and professional problems. Memos passed backwards and forwards when a personal visit or a telephone call from the General would have done the trick, and as each memo was written, misunderstandings piled up. These futile exchanges of ideas usually resulted in one memo to the General simply not being answered, and you knew then that he wished the matter to be dropped. Not once in three years did he discuss my future or offer to take me out for a drink at the end of the day, nor did he suggest a lunch or drink or weekend at his country home to any other member of his staff. What was really worrying about this pattern of behaviour was that it emanated from a man charged with engineering good public relations, and as every professional practitioner of the art is only too well aware, a drink in El Vino's is worth twenty letters in the fivepenny post.

Part of the General's charm is his unworldliness, but surely this particular quality cannot qualify anyone for a job which should engage him in daily communication with the press. I am not even sure how it got him through the army. In view of the supposedly sexual nature of the articles I wrote which were later to be used as an excuse to have me sacked I recall with renewed incredulity a conversation I had with the General about a parish priest we both knew, who became psychologically unwell and was in serious need of pastoral help from his bishop. For some reason I now forget, this event lead the General's train of thought to some sexual incident he had had to deal with in the army, and in trying to recall the incident he had to ask me to remind him what buggery meant. The embarrassment with which he fumbled for the word was in itself embarrassing to me, and I remember marvelling that any senior staff officer, never mind a man whose life had been spent in the company of other men in many different countries of the world, could be so ignorant of the facts of life.

The General was incapable of hiding his ignorance. After a visit to St. Paul's Cathedral one night (Cardinal Heenan had been there to preach during the Week of Prayer for Christian Unity) I took

56

The Archbishop leaves the London School of Economics accompanied by his press officer, after an engagement the author describes as a complete fiasco in terms of seizing the advantage of a ready-made platform.

Photograph by The Guardian

Overleaf
Above
The Archbishop with his press officer on arrival at the airport in British Honduras during a tour of the Province of the Church of the West Indies in the spring of 1968. The author, who was just about to introduce a press conference for the Archbishop, is wearing what Mrs. Ramsey used to describe as his working face.

Below
Dr. Ramsey talks to Canon David Paton during a break between sessions of the Fourth Assembly of the World Council of Churches at Uppsala in July, 1968. The author is on the Archbishop's right, and beside him is the Bishop of Cariboo, who at the time was executive officer of the Anglican Communion.

the General to dinner at the Wig and Pen. On the way, I mentioned a journalist by name, which prompted the General to ask, "How do you get to know all these fellows; I mean, where do you actually meet them?" This exhibition of initiative hardly squared with the Bishop of London's bland assertion in the Church Assembly debate four years earlier that General Block had "the ability to make this contacts where he did not already possess them."

My own somewhat impatient and sometimes intolerant nature was perhaps too easily exacerbated by what I regarded as the General's obsession with trivial administrative details rather than broad and bold policy. As I saw it, he would waste his own time and the Church's money by solemnly putting on his bowler hat, taking up his umbrella and walking round to the Church Commissioners to discuss with the First Estates Commissioner, Sir Ronald Harris, a query on my expenses following a thirty day visit paid by the Archbishop to the Church of the Province of the West Indies. Both the General and Sir Ronald must have been on at least £4,500 a year. That constituted a £9,000 a year head-on collision on Millbank, at an estimated speed of 4.5 miles an hour (Sir Ronald was stationary at the time, actually sitting at his desk when the General 'burst' in). The expenses under fire amounted to £60 for two lightweight suits. The result was a grudging acceptance of a fait accompli, as the money had already been spent and the suits were hanging up in my wardrobe.

The General certainly spent far more of his time meeting his fellow top brass in the establishment than he did members of the press. In the three years I worked with him I never knew him to initiate a piece of news. Basically he seems to believe that press officers exist to release press handouts, and I do not think he can say that he counts a single journalist among his personal friends. Had he adapted the running of his office strictly according to his own limitations all might have been well, but he suffers from a fatal inability to interfere at some stage or other in areas he has led his subordinates to believe he has handed over to them.

As it slowly dawned on the General that he had lost control over the Archbishop's public relations he saw pastures new at Bishopsthorpe. In preparation for a visit the Archbishop of York was due to make to South Africa, during which the Archbishop planned to mix business with pleasure, choosing South Africa as a country in which to have a holiday because of the sun, General Block spent some days drafting a press release; when I saw the release just before it was due to go out I judged it totally incompetent, and as the General was away that day I was faced with the decision whether to let it slide, thus risking a drop in the C.I.O's. reputation in Fleet Street, or rewording it, knowing that if I did so it would be virtually impossible to justify my action to the General. I took the latter course, and the General flew into one of his rare rages. I can quite see why. If I was to continue trying to raise the level of professionalism in the C.I.O., he was in the end going to be left high and dry, for while I do not claim that I was the perfect professional I do believe that he was the perfect amateur. Soon there would be nothing left for him to do but refuse to sign my expenses.

There was a sequel to the Archbishop of York's visit to South Africa. In the previous December Dr. Coggan had said, "I think it is an awful pity when politics get into sport. The motives of the demonstrators may be praiseworthy but their methods are not. Perhaps it is because the wrong people are carrying the banners. I personally believe it has all got out of hand." Not unreasonably, Dr. Coggan's remarks were taken to mean that it was all right for the South African government to segregate sportsmen for political reasons but all wrong for people in this country to protest about it. His use of the phrase "the wrong people" was unfortunate. At the time of the proposed Springboks tour four of the wrong people turned out to be his fellow bishops.

The Archbishop was due back from South Africa early on a Saturday morning. Despite Dr. Coggan's unhappy touch with South African affairs I discovered that General Block was planning to hold a press conference for him at Church House at half-past-nine in the morning. Few journalists relish being summoned to a press conference at nine-thirty in the morning at the best of times. To be summoned at that hour on a Saturday could only indicate that Dr. Coggan had something so momentous to say that the Sunday newspapers could be expected to carry it on their front pages. As it happened, the General had not even found out whether the Archbishop had anything to say or not.

In the nick of time I was able to point out to the General the folly of calling a press conference under such conditions, especially as I felt that the less publicity given to Dr. Coggan's South African venture the better. The General accepted my advice and there was no press conference — until the Archbishop reached the safety of

Bishopsthorpe, when without consultation with the C.I.O. and indeed in direct contradiction to the advice he had been given, he suddenly gave a press conference of his own. During the course of it he said the Springboks were regarded as heroes, which was a nice piece of free publicity for Dr. Vorster. He also went on record as saying that Dr. Vorster would liberalise the South African regime, but at no time did he condemn apartheid, which produced from the Bishop of Southwark the perfectly reasonable retort that he did not know how one could liberalise something that was inherently evil.

In the event, I had been wasting my time in trying to hammer some commonsense into the General's P.R. programme for the Archbishop of York, and indeed I wonder now if I was not simply hammering one more nail into my own coffin.

CHAPTER FOUR

SEX IS A FOUR-LETTER WORD

Oh we don't want to lose you
But we think you ought to go :
First World War recruiting song.

I HAVE tried as fairly and impartially as possible, but obviously it has not been easy to be fair, and it has been impossible to be entirely impartial, to sketch in some of the events and personalities involved in my appointment as press officer to the Archbishop of Canterbury. The events that led to my dismissal are in my opinion bizarre, but I will try to record them accurately. Those Christians who take the ultimately, but somewhat unworldly, eternal view of events on this earth, believing that no matter how stupidly we behave God will somehow always get us out of the mess, and that however long the results of what we do may linger in temporal memories they don't really matter because those results occupy a mere day in the life of God, will of course shrug off my dismissal and the events surrounding it as of little importance in the total Eternal Plan. However, for historians of the here and now and for students of human behaviour, and indeed for those Christians who believe that time is not necessarily on the side of the Church, they may on the other hand possess a certain interest, and even perhaps a lesson or two for the future.

What happened was that I preached a dialogue sermon at the Church of St. John the Baptist, Hove, and I wrote an article for *Forum* and an article for *New Society*, and in the sermon and in both articles I touched, with varying emphasis, on the subject of sex. By preaching and writing freelance articles I was never in breach of my contract, for indeed I had no contract; I was on three months' notice, and that was all. Had I been in breach of a contract by freelancing the matter would have been perfectly simple. I should presumably have been sacked, and upon unquestionable grounds. Had I written articles on baking cakes, I doubt whether I should have been sacked. But I wrote articles on sexual topics, and I was sacked, and I was able to be sacked because I was working under an ad hoc system, a system under which I had no idea how I was doing until the umpire, who was making up the rules, suddenly shouted, "Out!"

It can of course be argued that I should not have been so naive as to write about sex while working for the Church, and that even though I was not forbidden to freelance I should have used greater discretion in my choice of subject or platform. If this argument is tenable then the onus is upon the Church to explain why sex as such is taboo, or at any rate what it was that I said and wrote that was for any reason so unacceptable to Christian doctrine that by holding and publicising the views and the facts which I did I proved myself literally unemployable. The sermon and the two articles in question are printed in full as appendices.

The sermon was preached on the First Sunday in Lent, 1970; I spoke for about twenty-five minutes, and I mentioned sex for about two minutes. What I said was this: "There is a grave danger that the gap between society and the Church is going to continue to widen. For example, during the next ten years I see immense and belated strides being made in the scientific and psychological study of sexuality in relation to the human personality, and it seems to me absolutely vital that the Church should tackle without delay the working out of a new theology of sex. To say officially that sexual relations are morally permissible only within the marriage of heterosexual partners is to beg a whole host of theological questions."

With hindsight, I rather regret the way in which I phrased this passage, with the particular emphasis I appeared to give to the marriage of heterosexual partners. I thought I was being clever by being precise, because I meant to imply that heterosexual relations should not necessarily be permitted only within marriage, but inevitably, I suppose, the passage came to be interpreted primarily as a plea for the official acceptance of homosexual relationships. In a way, I do not mind this interpretation being placed upon the passage too, because I also believe that in certain circumstances the Church should recognise the morality of homosexual partnerships, but this was not actually the specific point I was trying to make.

On their own initiative the parish advertised the sermon; the Overseas Service of the B.B.C. told me they had made arrangements to record it, and as in any case no preaching engagement can ever be regarded as a private occasion I thought it best to distribute the full text to the press, so that if they decided that anything in it was worth publishing they would not have to rely on a local newspaper reporter. I wrote to both the Archbishop and General Block explaining the situation, and I sent them both copies of the sermon.

While I was on a visit to the Bishop of Norwich to talk to a meeting of local newspaper and radio editors, General Block telephoned to say that the Archbishop wished me to delete the passage about sex. I explained that to delete a passage about sex once the press had received an advance script would invite rather more comment than the passage itself; very reluctantly, he accepted this advice but stressed that I was to say in the pulpit that I was speaking on my own behalf, not the Archbishop's! In the event, the sermon attracted most interest in the local and Church press. However, *The Daily Telegraph* did tag a brief reference to my remark about the need for a new theology of sex beneath a longer story headed "Sex Obsession Attacked by Dr. Heenan," in which the Cardinal's pastoral letter on Lenten Penance recorded Dr. Heenan as saying, "Anything to do with sex is published and debated as if it was the real centre of Catholic interest." When Dr. Ramsey saw me the following week he had this cutting in his hand, and rather amusingly, and with some justification, led me to believe that it proved that he understood more about public relations than I did, for just the very thing he had feared had come to pass; the press had identified me with himself and had used my remarks to draw a contrast between his views on sexual matters and the Cardinal's. During this interview the Archbishop was very kind and understanding, and said several times that he did not wish to censure me over what I said or wrote in a private capacity, but he was anxious that I should understand the danger that anything I did write or say might be construed as representing his own views.

Interestingly enough, I received a letter from a journalist on the *Sunday Telegraph* saying, "It was good to see a small note about you in *The Daily Telegraph* on Monday . . . . . I did think, however, that the Cardinal Heenan story got undue prominence . . . . . we journalists really do have our priorities wrong!"

Following my interview with the Archbishop I wrote to him confirming that I understood his anxieties, and in this letter I thought it right to tell him that I had recently been commissioned to write an article for *Forum*, on the subject of the permissive society. I described *Forum* to him as a serious, and in my view very valuable, publication, producing a monthly series of articles on many different aspects of sex and psychology. I went on to tell him that the editor was planning to say that I was press officer to the Archbishop of Canterbury but was writing in my private capacity and was expressing only my own views. However, I suggested that the Archbishop might wish all mention of my job deleted, and I said I was sure the editor would be willing to co-operate.

When the Archbishop received this letter he asked to see me, and told me in no uncertain terms that I was being naive. He said I was too well known as his press officer for it to matter one scrap whether I was billed as his press officer or not.

All letters written in the office went into a 'float' file and were circulated internally, so I had made no secret of the fact that I was writing for *Forum*; however, when General Block saw my letter to the Archbishop referring to *Forum* he saw fit to send a back-number to the Archbishop without discussing the matter with me. Sex, the Archbishop now kept telling me, was an inflammatory subject, and *Forum* was pornographic. I told the Archbishop I did not believe for one moment that *Forum* was pornographic; on the contrary, it was trying to help people with sexual and emotional problems who would not go anywhere near the Church for help because either the Church ignored their problems or it had no solutions to them. The editor had asked me to write because he wanted his readers to know that at least some Christians were concerned about these matters.

The Archbishop was kind enough to say that he thought I had complete integrity but my judgment about what I could do privately while working for him was not always sound; my job was to protect him, not to cause him unnecessary worry. I offered to show him the *Forum* article, but he declined to see it. I offered to try and have it withdrawn, despite my reluctance to draw attention to the Archbishop's fear of articles about sex, and he said that on balance he would like it withdrawn, if this could be done discreetly, on the grounds that he did not like the idea of a member of his staff writing in *Forum*. He reiterated his refusal to act as a censor, and said I must continue to use my own discretion.

The Archbishop showed me a letter he had received from someone complaining about my sermon, and he told me he intended to reply by saying I had been naive. This seemed to me to be an exact reinactment of his reaction to criticism of the brochure *Lambeth '68.*

As the Archbishop was obviously so perturbed at the prospect of my writing anything to do with sex I thought it right at this interview to tell him that I had also recently had an article accepted by *New Society* on a sexual theme. Oh, he said, that was perfectly all right, a different matter entirely; *New Society* was a highly reputable magazine. The Archbishop was later to deny all recollection of this part of our conversation.

I left the Archbishop's study feeling terribly depressed. There was no one in the Palace to whom I felt I could talk. I got on the train for Hove, where I live, and went straight to the bar. I ordered a whisky, and scribbled out my resignation on the back of a postcard. Halfway to Brighton a young lad of 19 bounced into the buffet, came straight up to me, and said "Hello." I said I was sorry but I did not think I knew him. "No," he said, "you don't, but I know you; I was in St. John's Church when you preached your sermon." He was kind enough to say the sermon had meant a good deal to him and to his parents, because apparently I had been talking about things that really mattered to them. His enthusiasm for life, and his apparent approval of what I had been trying to say, so cheered me up that I forgot my self-pity and tore up my resignation.

The next day I telephoned *Forum*, to discover that my article had already gone to press. I wrote a letter to the Archbishop, in which I said I had come to believe that he had a perfect right to impose censorship upon me, which was to say that I believed he had a perfect right to ask me not to engage in journalism or public speaking while I was his press officer, but that I would find it irrational to be censored only on the subject of sex. However, as he had chosen not to exercise any censorship at all I would continue to use my own discretion, as this was his wish. I also told him I felt that for me to ask the editor of *Forum* to suppress my article once the issue had gone to press would cause more dismay than was likely to be caused when the article appeared, but I had obtained the editor's consent to withdraw any reference to my job, and not to advertise the article in any way or to bring it directly to the attention of newspapers.

As far as the letters of complaint about my sermon were concerned, I told the Archbishop I felt it my duty to point out that whatever he might think privately about my conduct it could not possibly reflect to his benefit if he expressed criticism about me to people outside his household. In reply, I received a letter from the Archbishop in his own hand, saying, "Thank you for your kind and thoughtful endeavour to prevent your article in *Forum* from bringing any difficulty to me. I much appreciate your action. In answering the few letters I have had as a result of your dialogue sermon I shall omit any criticism of you."

These events were taking place between February 12th — 26th. Nothing more occurred until my article appeared in *New Society* on June 4th. The Archbishop is said to have received letters of complaint about this article, although no one at Lambeth Palace seems able to say how many letters. The Archbishop spoke to me about the article in great agitation, and what particularly impressed him was that he had received a letter of complaint from Mr. Brian Roberts, editor of the *Sunday Telegraph*. At the same time he had in his possession a cutting, again given to him by General Block without my knowledge, from John Gordon's column in the *Sunday Express*, expressing typical Beaverbrook indignation at a former member of Church Assembly writing in *Forum*, but making no mention of my name or my present job.

I explained to the Archbishop that I regarded the complaint from Mr. Roberts as completely untypical of the attitude of Fleet Street in general; Mr. Roberts comes from a right-wing ecclesiastical family (his brother was formerly editor of the *Church Times*), and I had good reason to know that he had not been happy when some months previously I had not been too keen on recommending an interview by the Archbishop for the *Sunday Telegraph* in relation to a general survey they were making of the Church of England. Nevertheless, the Archbishop became convinced that Fleet Street was taking notice of what I was saying and writing as a private person. At this interview the Archbishop appeared entirely unaware that I had an article due to appear in *New Society*, and I had great difficulty in persuading him to believe that I had gone out of my way to warn him that such an article was due to appear. More important, I told him I would not write again on sexual topics as long as I worked for him, and in a letter I wrote the following day I reaffirmed this promise, describing it as a willingly self-imposed form of censorship. At no time did the Archbishop give me any reason to believe that he had not gladly accepted my assurance on this matter.

Four weeks later, Church Assembly was due to meet for its summer session. During that session, which lasted from Tuesday, July 7th to Thursday, July 9th, General Block gave one of a series of working lunches for half-a-dozen bishops, to tell them about the work of the Church Information Office. As usual, I was invited to this lunch, at which the Archdeacon of Chester took the chair, and I was asked to tell the bishops about the press work of the C.I.O. The Archdeacon behaved towards me as though I was still a respected and permanent member of the staff. So did the General, who throughout the course of that week continued to discuss long-term plans with me, and to seek my advice on routine matters. On the Tuesday, the Assembly debated their budget, including an allocation of £56,180 for the Church Information Office. On the final day, at noon, the Archbishop was due to make a speech winding up the Assembly. I prepared to have it released to the press, but that morning I was tipped off by John Redfern of the *Daily Express* that Miss Eva Bestley had reported every session of Church Assembly for the past fifty years. I wrote a memo to the Archbishop suggesting that he might like to mention this fact in his speech, and handed the memo to him at the rostrum. He looked up at me as he took the memo from my hand, and his face was what I can only describe as a complete blank. I sat for a moment beside his domestic chaplain, and I said to him, "Do you know, the Archbishop has just looked at me as though he has never seen me before in his life!"

When he came to deliver his speech the Archbishop interpolated a charming reference to Miss Bestley, and mentioned in general terms his appreciation of the services rendered to the Assembly by the press, a thought which had not occurred to him when he first wrote his speech. These remarks brought forth the longest applause from the Assembly on anything the Archbishop said in his speech. It was, thanks to John Redfern, the last service I was ever to perform for the Archbishop. I had arranged with General Block to have the following day off, but he asked if I would come into the office specially as he wished to see me on a matter of urgency. When I kept the appointment he apologised for bringing me up from Brighton on my day off, especially as he had to tell me that on the following Monday I would be receiving a letter from the Central Board of Finance terminating my employment.

I could not believe the Archbishop had not been consulted, but as a matter of course I asked for confirmation of this, and the General nodded. He also told me that Sir John Scott and the Archdeacon of Chester had been consulted, but in a letter to me Sir John denies that he was consulted. As Sir John, the Archdeacon and the General have all declined to give me an interview, and as the Archbishop failed to take into his confidence his senior chaplain, the Bishop of Maidstone, it is now impossible to tell for certain who was consulted. But at some time during the four weeks between approximately June 4th and July 7th General Block asked the Archbishop's permission to sack me, and presumably the Archbishop gave his consent. The delay in sacking me between the writing, publication and comments upon the offending articles, and the day after Church Assembly had gone home, can only be accounted for by a political desire to avoid the possibility of questions being asked in Church Assembly during the finance debate. So Church Assembly, who five years earlier had seen fit to question General Block's appointment, was deliberately denied the opportunity of questioning his dismissal of the Archbishop of Canterbury's personal press officer.

Not only had the Archbishop of Canterbury received an assurance from me that I would not write on sexual subjects again so long as I worked for him, but General Block and I had discussed the matter exhaustively, and while agreeing to differ on the main issues, the General had never given me any indication that he believed the matter was one so serious that I should have to be dismissed. He had also seen copies of all my letters to the Archbishop, so that he knew how matters had been left between the Archbishop and myself. What arguments General Block employed with the Archbishop I do not know; my guess is that he managed to persuade him that as a so-called radical I was just too dangerous to have around.

The General was vague about the reasons for my dismissal and the terms on which I was leaving; I had to press him on both matters before he would definitely say that I was being sacked, and that I was being sacked because my judgment was at fault over what I could write in a private capacity. I asked whether he had not considered advising the Archbishop to ask me to look for another job and then to resign. Apparently the idea had never occurred to him. When I said that I thought from a public relations point of view, never mind a humanitarian one, it would have been the sensible thing to do, he said, "But you wouldn't have resigned, would you." I told him that of course I would, to which he replied, "You amaze me!"

The General then suggested that on the following Monday we should sit down and draft an agreed press release announcing that I was leaving, but he did not seem to have any idea as to what the release should say. In view of subsequent developments, he did however add what I now regard as a sinister remark, to the effect that once the release had gone out (and he suggested that we should embargo it for the following Thursday!) I would of course be entirely free to say anything I liked to the press. I asked the General who would be looking after the Archbishop's press relations in future, and in particular to whom I should direct routine press enquiries over the weekend, now that it was clearly impossible for me to act as press officer while I was under notice. Again, this was a matter to which he did not appear to have given any consideration, and after a pause he said that he would himself be looking after the Archbishop. How on earth I was supposed to refer the press to the General for the next six days without journalists wondering what was going on I do not know!

The Archbishop was due to leave for a visit to South Africa on November 12th, and I had already done a lot of work in preparation for the visit. I did not believe that as a press officer I was indispensable, but I could hardly believe that the Archbishop intended to go on such a delicate mission without a press officer of some sort. When I asked General Block if he had given any consideration to this matter, he replied, "South Africa has got nothing to do with it."

Turning to my immediate problems, having just sacked me at three months' notice the General said he was sorry I was going as I had always served both the Archbishop and himself efficiently and loyally, and he added that he wanted to do anything he could to help me! He thought for example that I might prefer to leave the office without serving my three months' notice. He also said he knew that I had not been very well lately, and he thought that three months of not travelling up to London by train might help me to get better!

By this time I was ready for the cup of coffee *The People* later wrote about in a piece of amusing Sunday knockabout journalism! Having had my coffee I took the first train back to Brighton. I did so because primarily I was extremely shaken by the fact that the Archbishop had not seen me himself to tell me that he wished me to leave; with hindsight, I shall always blame myself for not telephoning his chaplain immediately to ask to see Dr. Ramsey, because I think that if I had seen him myself, even at that late hour, I might have been able to warn him, for the third time, of the danger of failing to support his staff in public. After all, "Primate Sacks Press Officer Over Sex" was going to be a literally heaven-sent gift from General Block to Fleet Street. There is of course no guarantee that I should have succeeded in persuading the Archbishop to take a more rational course, but I wish now that I had at least made the attempt. So, I believe, does he. For just as there was a singular lack of communication between Lambeth Palace and Church House over my appointment, subsequent events have made me come to the conclusion that there was even less communication, with far more unhappy results, over my dismissal.

On my return home I realised that I had many things to do, letters to write, engagements to cancel, and so on. Feeling in need of relaxation I decided to have a sauna, and so on that Friday afternoon I went to a sauna bath to try and recover from the immediate shock of events. It was a fatal decision! Jack Tinker, a friend I had known for ten years, and a fellow journalist who was at the time on the *Brighton Evening Argus* but who was just about to join the *Daily Sketch*, happened to come into the sauna while I was there. As he was an old friend I naturally said that I had just been sacked. What never occurred to me was that he would telephone the *Daily Sketch* and sell them, for £20, a first-edition scoop, without first asking if to do so was all right by me.

And so on Sunday morning the *Daily Sketch* rang me up. The news was out. I confirmed that I had been sacked, and the *Sketch* then telephoned the Old Palace at Canterbury and General Block. The Archbishop's chaplain came on the telephone to me in a terrible flap, asking what he should do. I told him it was a bit late to ask for my advice, as I had just been sacked. "But you are still the Archbishop's press officer," poor Philip kept saying, "No," I tried to explain, "you had better get used to the idea that I am not the Archbishop's press officer, because the Archbishop has just sacked

me, and therefore I can hardly speak for the Archbishop, can I?"
"Can't you say, 'No comment',," he implored! Philip then went on
to tell me that I had no idea how upset the Archbishop and Mrs.
Ramsey were, and how only the evening before they had been
discussing how they could take me to South Africa with them, how
they could keep me on at Lambeth Palace instead of Church House,
and heaven knows what other fanciful ideas.

I was then telephoned by the General who was, as usual, dumb-
founded that the press had got a story; he had told the *Daily
Sketch* they could not possibly use the story about my sacking as he
had not yet informed his own staff! It had however occurred to the
General that there must have been a leak, and it had also occurred
to him that I must have been the source of it. I told the General
that naturally I had mentioned my sacking to a few personal
friends, and I asked him if he really expected me not to mention it
to a single person during the entire weekend. Without a moment's
hesitation he replied, "Yes".

In the long run of course the leak made no difference to the
press coverage of the event; it merely brought forward the publicity
by a few days. But the General went around telling everyone that
the enormous press coverage that followed was a direct result of
the leak. What the leak actually did was to make it finally impossible for me, even on the Monday, to ask the Archbishop to call off
the whole thing.

I knew that by about 10 p.m., when the first edition of the *Sketch*
landed on the news desks of every other paper in Fleet Street, my
telephone would start to ring. It rang for two hours. The *Sketch*
had run the story on the front page under the headline "Dr.,
Ramsey Sacks a Personal Adviser; PRIMATE IN SEX MAGA-
ZINE ROW". They quoted General Block as saying, "It is purely
a private matter!"

The *Daily Mirror* then cleared their front page, and ran the
story under the heading, "Dr. Ramsey's Press Aide Loses His
Job; PRIMATE SACKS AUTHOR OF SEX STORIES." The
Daily Express ran the story on the front page with a photograph of the
Archbishop, under the headline, "Primate's Adviser Fired Over Sex
Articles." *The Daily Telegraph* also placed the story on its front page,
under the headline, "Dr. Ramsey's Adviser Dismissed." *The Times*
and the *Daily Mail* both went on to the front page, *The Sun* ran
the story on an inside page, and *The Guardian* ran it on its back

news page. The B.B.C. asked me to record an interview for the *Today* programme, which I did at one o'clock in the morning from the Brighton Pavilion. My interview went out at about ten-past-seven in the morning, and by ten-to-eight I had been offered another job. I was also being photographed by the *Evening Standard* as I was getting dressed, and telephoned by *The Evening News* as I was leaving for the station. The Church was in the news.

By the time I reached my office it resembled a scene from an Ealing Studio comedy. Agency reporters and newspaper photographers were everywhere. I was filmed for television packing my brief case and unpacking it. The *Daily Sketch* telephoned to take me out to lunch because they wanted to commission an article. Diary writers were trying to follow up the biggest story of the silly season for their early afternoon editions, Southern Television wanted me to go to Southampton to broadcast but settled for a studio in London, and the Archbishop's chaplain telephoned to say that Dr. Ramsey would be pleased to see me at noon.

When I entered the Archbishop's study he said how grieved he was that I was leaving. I asked why he had not seen me himself before getting someone else to sack me, and he replied, "I thought I could be more help to you pastorally afterwards." When I enquired how that could possibly be he replied, "Well, I can't now, you are too bitter." He remarked that when he had read my article in *New Society* it had occurred to him that I was "riding for a fall," "trying to get the sack!" He added that he had "tried to save me," but that he had had to take General Block's advice.

My personal views on these comments are that presumably as Archbishop of Canterbury, Dr. Ramsey can "save" any member of his personal staff if he wishes to do so, and he certainly does not have to take anyone else's advice on anything. I have always understood that the top man in any job is paid the top salary to call upon advice if he wishes, and then to accept it or reject it on his own responsibility. As for the suggestion that I had been trying to get the sack, this remark left me literally speechless. The Archbishop looked distressed and uncomfortable, and kept glancing at the clock, obviously wishing the interview could end without ever having begun. Finally he said there seemed nothing to be added, and he got up to show me out, reiterating his grief that I was leaving.

It would be tedious to recapitulate the details of the press coverage that the story continued to receive for several weeks. Comments were made on television shows, and *The Evening News* drew attention to two pertinent facts: that Church Assembly had been denied an opportunity of debating the issue, and that several people in Whitehall as well as Lambeth would be keeping their fingers crossed until the Archbishop returned from South Africa. In *The Guardian* Geoffrey Moorhouse wrote an article analysing some of the factors that lay behind the facade of the situation, stating that the dismissal of the Archbishop of Canterbury's personal press officer was a much more complex issue than had so far been made out. In the course of writing the article he spoke on the telephone to the Archdeacon of Chester, chairman of the Church Information Advisory Committee, who had never met Mr. Moorhouse in his life but apparently thought it advisable to call him by his Christian name. "Bless you," he said to Mr. Moorhouse, "you know I'd do anything I possibly could to help you chaps, but sometimes there really comes a point when I think it's better to leave the whole thing in the hands of one chap."

The story travelled round the world, and was reported extensively in the British provincial press, including the *Brighton Evening Argus*, who kindly said in their headline that I "wasn't sacked over sex charges!" It was about the only fact they did get right, and this report, a mixture of inaccurate reporting and emotional verbiage contributed by myself under what by this time was becoming a bit of an emotional strain, certainly made me squirm when I read it. Otherwise, the press were very fair to me, and my own greatest grief was to see so much written and drawn that reflected the public's worst fears about the Church and its professional competence, and worse still, its lack of any true understanding of life.

In the Fleet Street papers, the *Daily Sketch* ran a cartoon in the middle of the week showing the Archbishop as a vicious man, kicking someone out of the Church. The *Daily Mail* ran a cartoon by Emmwood, which summed up the entire situation in a nutshell; the Archbishop was shown coming into the vestry with a copy of *Forum* in his hand, looking pretty angry. A choirboy was pointing to another choirboy and was saying, "Please Your Grace — Bottomley has just written an un-Christian word!" The word Bottomley had written on the wall was 'sex'.

The Times, *The Evening News* and *The Spectator* ran cartoons, and so, a week after the event, did *The Observer*. Dr. Cecil Northcott,

73

Church Correspondent of *The Daily Telegraph*, asked in a letter to his own newspaper whether I had been dismissed for writing a couple of independent articles or because those articles were on sex. He said my instant dismissal raised questions on which the facts should be published. Needless to say, this letter received no response from those who had sacked me.

Lord Beaumont of Whitley, while admitting an interest because he was a personal friend and a former employer of mine, registered "an emphatic protest" in the letter columns of the *Church Times*, and asked, "I do not know whether the worst aspect . . . is that the Church seems irredeemably stuck in that attitude to sex which is best summed up in the remark of Lord Fisher of Lambeth: 'I have found that, whatever else is to be said about sex as a topic, it need not occupy more than a very small proportion of a person's time and attention, and that, while it is easy to let it occupy more and more and become more and more engrossing, to do so distracts anyone very seriously from more healthy interests'." Lord Beaumont ended his letter by saying: "It may be that even worse, one man's career should be unwarrantedly and arbitrarily jeopardised by this attitude."

By the middle of the week, General Block began to realise that he was in the throes of a press story which was not exactly under his control. He moved into action in a somewhat mysterious way, by issuing one of his rare statements to the press — but only to the Church press — in which he solemnly made it clear that all the publicity about my sacking had not emanated from his office!

It had not indeed. It had emanated from Fleet Street, from men trained to recognise a story when they see one. It also stirred into action Bishop John Robinson, Dean, of Trinity College, Cambridge, who has been trained to recognise theological concerns in relation to society. In a letter to *The Guardian* Bishop Robinson placed my sacking in the context of three other contemporary actions which he regarded as ominous signs of the times. He wrote: "Now that the Conservative Party may, astonishingly, have been saved from itself over the folly of selling arms to South Africa, one could use the respite to reflect on some decisions of recent weeks. I instance four:

(1) The judgment on student violence at the Garden House, Cambridge. The swingeing sentences, particularly the mindless recommendations for deportation, combined with Mr. Justice

74

Melford Stevenson's gratuitous slur on the senior members of the university, were calculated as nothing else could have been to produce precisely the opposite effect to what he intended.

(2) The manner of the arrest and imprisonment of Miss Bernadette Devlin, when she was actually on her way to give herself up, seems similarly to have been almost inspired to turn her into a martyr.

(3) The blunt sacking by General Block of Mr. Michael De-la-Noy from the Church Information Office, when he himself has said he would willingly have looked for another job, looks a classic exercise in the communications industry of how not to win friends and influence people.

(4) Finally, we turn to Sir Alec Douglas-Home's antics which leave one breathless to think that a British Government has found a policy which seems thick and insensitive even to an administration which includes Mr. Spiro T. Agnew.

"All these were decisions made by honourable, older men of the Right in dealing with a world which they reveal they simply do not understand. The lessons seem to be: (a) the risk we run of having such men in executive, administrative, or judicial positions from which they can exercise such unchecked power over the future; and (b) the enormous vigilance required, and, thank God, forthcoming from the community at large to ensure that such sheer stupidity is counter-productive even of its own counter-productivity."

I was overwhelmed by letters and telephone calls from journalists with generous offers of help, from personal friends I had not seen for many years, and from complete strangers, expressing dismay and sympathy. I think a few paragraphs from a selection of these letters are worth printing because the comments made do seem to reflect attitudes towards the Church and life that never occur to the establishment. They demonstrate the dangerous gulf that so often exists between those who make decisions and those who receive them.

A freelance journalist wrote to say, "I was shocked to read of your dismissal and all I can say is that I am very, very sorry. It sounds to me like a shocking case of intolerance. Please let me know if I can be of help in any way. I have built up over the years a large number of freelance contacts and it is possible that some of them may be of use to you."

75

A radical young Christian layman wrote, "I was saddened to see the unfortunate news about your job in the papers this week. I read your article in *New Society* some months ago and thought it a particularly brave and sensitive piece of writing — though I never for a minute imagined you would reap burning coals etc. as a result."

A priest from an overseas chaplaincy wrote, "I just wish to put on record my sorrow and indignation at your dismissal, and to express to you my fullest support and sympathy. Of the two articles involved I read the one in *Forum* and felt myself in substantial agreement with it."

A parish priest from the Rochester diocese wrote, "I am sorry that this has happened to you and that you are added to the list of establishment casualties. It becomes increasingly difficult to work for a firm which appears to be content to argue about theology and avoid real issues."

A layman from Kingston-upon-Thames made the following point: "Heaven knows why the Church, in common with many people both inside and outside it, should regard an interest in sex in all its forms so reprehensible, but it is so. To my mind violence, mental cruelty and a disregard for the sanctity of life are the true obscenities of our time, but the Church still evidently holds up its hands in horror at the dreadful impiety of an interest in sex, our most basic instinct."

A Roman Catholic freelance journalist was kind enough to write, "I don't care whether you've been imprudent or not: all I do know is that Lambeth Palace has lost a damned good press officer, one who has attracted the approval and admiration of many in my Church. Fifteen years ago I would have said it was time you came over to Rome. If we all speak differently today, it is in no small measure due to the work of people like yourself. This then is simply an expression of solidarity with you at this trying time, and to assure you that you have many Catholic well-wishers. If I can be of any service to you, at this time, please do not hesitate to let me know. This goes beyond the normal conventional bleat. I would really be glad to help, and although only a minnow myself I do know quite a lot of whales."

A priest who is also headmaster of a Church of England school wrote, "I know the 'offending' articles and found them sensible and helpful; but even if they had not been so I should consider the treatment you have now received bigoted, puritanical and sadly typical of a firm with which one wants less and less to be associated."

A young ordinand in his first year at a theological college wrote to say, "If the Church is to make an impact she must lose her 'damned respectability'."

One final quotation must do. It comes from a letter which stays most vividly in my mind, and it comes from the only letter which I received anonymously. I think the Church would do well to ponder on this letter and to hang its head in shame. It said, "I have just read of your sacking. I felt that I must write at once to tell you that I am very sorry that this had to happen to you. I want you to know that I admire you for the stand you have taken. I think you are a very brave man. I have only one regret, that I feel I have to remain anonymous for obvious reasons. I wish that I could write or talk to you with absolute freedom on this subject that is to so many a dirty word.

"I am a professing and very active Christian and try to live accordingly but I am afraid that I have homosexual tendencies which make me compelled to live a form of double life. This state of affairs causes me great concern at times and I often wish that I could talk to another responsible Christian follower about it."

If this man is a very active Christian presumably he is a member of a parish, yet he has to write to a complete stranger, which seems to me a terrible indictment of the parish in which he lives.

So much for the views of the world. Meanwhile, back at Church House General Block, who is said to have been looking a little stunned for a day or two, pulled himself together sufficiently to suggest that he was the chap to go to South Africa. As adverse publicity mounted so he entrenched himself mentally, coming to believe with greater and greater conviction as each day slid by that the advice he had given the Archbishop had been for the best. He continued to blame me for the leak to the *Daily Sketch* and clung to the pathetic belief that somehow or other all would have been well if a press release about my dismissal had gone out from the C.I.O. Had I wished to leak the story myself I should of course have sold it to the *News of the World* for £100, not to the *Daily Sketch* for the measly £20 they paid Jack Tinker!

General Block's views about the desirability of getting rid of me may well have been shared by others like him in the shires, for whom sex is still a four-letter word. It was not however shared by everyone in the Church. After a series of telephone calls and 'soundings', the suggestion was made to Lambeth Palace that only by a swift, imaginative and courageous decision to recall me could the Archbishop redeem his own and the Church's reputation for moral courage and commonsense. It was also put to Lambeth that such an act could prove a major breakthrough for public life in this country, by a leading figure admitting he had made a mistake. Whether the suggestion ever reached the ears of the Archbishop I do not know. I am told that it got short shrift from those prominent members of the establishment who had it in their power to advise the Archbishop on a method of healing the breach made in relations between the Church and the world and between the Church Information Office and Fleet Street.

However, exactly seven days after being sacked I did receive a letter from the Archbishop. It ran to three pages, and was written in his own hand. It is very personal, but I have the Archbishop's permission to paraphrase it. He wrote to say that during the week, with more time to give his mind to it all, he had come to realise that a great blunder had been made, involving injustice to me and unnecessary damage to himself. He had slipped badly, he reproached himself bitterly, and he asked my forgiveness.

It was a sad and generous letter. It was moving in its Christian dependence upon charity. It was revealing of even the Archbishop's apparent impotence to match actions with words in the face of opposition from an establishment collectively more powerful than perhaps he had ever realised. It was a letter no secular employer would have dared to write without offering to re-employ someone he thought had been unjustly sacked. All in all, it was the slightly unreal culmination of the silliest set of circumstances any novelist could ever have dreamed up in order to bring to a personally agonising end the three most enjoyable years of my life.

CHAPTER FIVE

THE FUTURE?

In an expanding universe, time is on the side of the outcast:
Quentin Crisp, *The Naked Civil Servant.*

THE ecclesiastical establishment is at present a necessary evil; I believe it could become a power for good. But there can be only one justification for the institutional Church; it should exist to enable people to practise Christianity effectively, but most effective Christian work and witness in this country is carried out despite the institutional Church, not because of it.

I say the establishment is a necessary evil not because I believe the men and women who constitute the establishment are themselves evil — far from it — but because they work in a rarified bureaucratic atmosphere that tends to bring out the worst in them rather than the best. It fosters a greed for good living (bishops' tables may not be groaning with goodies but 11 diocesan bishops still live in castles or palaces), it encourages an enjoyment of pomp and ceremony for its own sake, and most dangerous of all it too easily enables its members to preach Christianity in a kind of vacuum. It is so simple for a bishop or a dean or a lay member of the General Synod to make speeches attacking racial prejudice, advocating pastoral aid for homosexuals, denouncing slums, but very few members of the establishment are ever going to get their own hands dirty, even doing the washing up. Deans are worrying themselves silly about raising enough money to keep the cathedral roof in repair, never mind a roof over their own heads; the dearth of intellectual appointments to deaneries in recent years has been because few men of the right calibre can afford to live in sprawling 18th century deaneries, and prefer to educate their children on the

79

living wage they can earn in a university. And diocesan bishops seem frozen into a pathological inability to delegate the administrative burden of running their diocese in order to be ready at a moment's notice to act as a real Father-in-God to their clergy, many of whom are men broken in spirit and too proud or too humble to admit it.

And all this means that the standard of the Church's leadership is dismally low. In the 19th century age of gaiters, when bishops rode around their dioceses, and despite the industrial revolution life still moved at a pace most men could cope with, the staid and wise old prelate had a valuable and respected place in society. Today, the leaders of the Church are up against modern methods of communication a bit more demanding than the sermon. For better or worse, people take their impression of the Church — or of any other organisation — from what they see on television or hear on the wireless or read in the newspapers about its leaders. It does not matter what a bishop is doing or saying in the privacy of his own home, his public image — and that of the Church — will inevitably be conditioned by what people think he is doing and saying. They will judge the sort of person he is by how he appears in public.

This is why it was such a farce that through a hamfisted piece of public relations General Block and the Archbishop of Canterbury between them were able to project a disastrous impression of insensitivity and unworldliness when they sacked me instead of asking me to look for another job. They compounded their error by choosing sex as the battleground, not so much because sex is in itself intrinsically titillating or interesting, but because the Church's attitude towards sex is of such astonishing interest and concern to society.

The Church, after all, has had a lot to do with the building up of society's own attitudes to sex, which are mostly ridden with guilt and fear. When the Church demonstrated that it was afraid of sex to the extent of having to get rid of me it merely confirmed the belief so many people hold, that the Church is not remotely worried about the real problems that worry ordinary people.

What the Church believes about sex, whether it is prepared to spell it out in words of one syllable or not, is that absolutely all physical sexual activity is taboo outside marriage. It makes this rule despite the fact that man is the most highly sexed animal within that creation the Church believes God created. What the Church leaves unexplained is what God intended man to do with his sexual nature before marriage or in the event of never getting married. And there is quite a lot of explaining to do. From the age of 12 or 13 the hormones are simply racing round our bodies, and most medical opinion today asserts that celibacy, except for those who have a genuine vocation to it, and they are very few indeed, is both physically and pyschologically harmful.

For emotional reasons too I should have thought it was fairly clear that man was not a naturally celibate animal. Somewhat belatedly, the Church has at least come to accept that sexual activity within marriage is morally permissible not just for the procreation of the species but for the mutual enjoyment of the partners; in other words, the Church has come to accept, even if it does not realise it has, that essentially sexual activity is an attempt, even if it is destined ultimately always to be an unsuccessful attempt, to break down the separate will, to destroy the terrible loneliness inseparable from the human condition.

Men and women are terribly lonely, for essentially they feel they are the centre of the universe, and ultimately completely alone. I do not expect the Church to advocate wholesale permissiveness or promiscuity in order to overcome this problem of loneliness. What we do need is a realistic balance between the demands of man's physical and emotional nature and the Church's guilt-ridden fear of sex of any kind outside marriage. Until the Church accepts the existence of the problem, and shows some signs of trying to come to terms with it, it will have little to offer those who crave assurance that the God of Christianity is indeed a God of love, and not a practical joker with a warped sense of humour.

Of course, sex was only the final excuse the establishment required in order to rid itself of someone whom, because of their own deep insecurity, they actually believed was a threat to them. First of all, there is in the Church a long-standing tradition of amateurism, and for better or worse I was hired as a professional. If a professional is working with amateurs there comes a time, however politely he may put it, when he has to tell them how things should be run. And for all the lip service paid in recent years to the rôle of the laos, the clergy do not much care for being told how to run their own show, still less do they really believe in their hearts there is a rôle for the laity. And for the time being, the Church has clearly come down in favour of continuing to run its own affairs in an amateur way.

Again, I was only 33 when I was appointed press officer to the Archbishop, and I have no doubt that the pathetic age *versus* youth syndrome went into play as well. Financially, I was earning as much as a diocesan bishop, and twice as much as most parish priests. That too can hardly have endeared me to a profession which cannot make up its mind whether to make a stand for holy poverty or to start a trade union. Finally, it is well-known that I enjoyed the privilege of a close personal relationship with the Archbishop and Mrs. Ramsey, when so few other people, and particularly so few members of the establishment, are in the same fortunate position.

The Church panicked, and it was sex that made its itchy finger pull the trigger, for basically the Church still equates sex with sin. For me to have written about sex — no matter what I said — was, in the eyes of the establishment, to have lain the Archbishop open to criticism for employing me. If the Church is nothing but a diplomatic agency, then I have every sympathy with this argument, and it was right that I should have been sacked. But if the Church is the vehicle through which men and women are asked to accept the existence of a God who created every single facet of human life I find the singling out of sex as the one subject that is forever taboo neurotic in the extreme.

As far as the Archbishop himself is concerned, he fell foul in public of his own deep-seated fear of attack. How he could ever have been allowed to drag the Church into his own personal psychological problems by those whose duty it was to advise him to keep his head I shall always find it very hard to understand.

I remember interviewing Archbishop Fisher when he was, he told me, 78½. At the end of an hour of perfectly serious discussion I asked the Archbishop, as I was leaving, what he believed was the most important single issue facing his successor. Without a moment's hesitation he replied, "Stop silly people rocking the boat".

But I believe that the boat has got to be rocked a good deal more in future if the Christian message of love, hope and forgiveness is to come across to a nation increasingly sceptical of the Church's concern for the issues that perplex and concern ordinary people. I am not saying I have all the answers, but in sacking me the Church showed that it had none, for what it demonstrated was a desperate lack of moral courage. It did not require of me any courage to write the articles for *Forum* and *New Society*, or to promise not to write any more articles of a similar nature; it would have required a certain amount of moral courage for the establishment to support me in public — as any self-respecting secular employer would have done — and the Church failed itself. In failing itself, it showed how little it understands the world it exists to serve.

The Church proclaims a gospel of love. But unless the Church is actually seen to love people nobody is going to understand the point of the Cross when every Easter some poor parson tries to drive it home. There is a desperate need for organisations that really do love people and care about them, which is to say, who actually do something about their condition. Increasingly, people are turning to the welfare services and charities for such love and care. And who can blame them? The whole point about being a bishop is that you have a ready-made platform for proclaiming the gospel of love through personal actions. Christ could have written 1,000 books about the need to meet people's needs where people are and when the needs arise, but no-one would have been impressed; instead, he took a bowl and washed his own disciples' feet.

What the Church lacks as well as a loving spirit is imagination. As the political power of the established Church wanes with each new wave of unexciting appointments to the episcopal bench so paradoxically its prestige increases, for the English seem particularly drawn towards the impotent. The Royal Family have never been so popular since they relinquished power, the trade unions never so unpopular since they took it over. What the Church has failed to realise is that unencumbered by the need to maintain the niceties of polite behaviour it has a new and possibly final chance to behave in public as it preaches in private. The hypocrisy and cowardice of the established religion of this realm is really frightening. During the three years I worked for the Archbishop of Canterbury I served in one way or another, either personally or professionally, no less than 42 other diocesan bishops, with some of whom I stayed, and others I entertained in my own home. When the axe fell, precisely two of these bishops took the trouble to write to me. Even if the other 40 had thought I had been a damned fool, could they not have written a postcard saying, "You have been a damned fool, but you are in my thoughts and prayers." What on earth do they think Christianity is all about? What on earth do they think personal relationships are all about? It was as though the favourite at a mediaeval court had fallen from grace, and had, automatically, to be deserted.

The bishops are frightened men because they are insecure, and they are insecure because they believe the *raison d'etre* for their existence is crumbling away. But this simply is not true. What is happening is that the Church in which they have been consecrated to act as the servants of the servants of Christ, in direct descent to the Apostles themselves, is changing its nature while they are sitting around talking together for hours on end about matters of interest to no-one but themselves. What they seem incapable of comprehending is that despite the established nature of the Church of England it is operating today, or it certainly should be operating, in a missionary situation.

In the old-fashioned sense of the word, England is a pagan country. Its culture may be Christian, but you do not clamber into heaven on the achievements of the past, you get there under modern conditions or not at all. The appointments to diocesan bishoprics are still based far too much on a desire to keep a steady balance between high and low, parish priest and principal, radical and conservative, when what is needed, in the broad interests of the Church, are men chosen on their own individual merits, not so much as equalising members of a team but as saints set on fire with enthusiasm; men prepared to rock the boat by stating in positive terms the reality of the gospel as it applies to urban boredom, industrial squalor, racial prejudice, unbearable noise, political cynicism, environmental pollution and the lunatic squandering of human and financial resources on lunar exploration.

When only 2 per cent of the country still goes to church we need bishops who will pledge themselves never to allow the building of another church in their diocese, who will foster instead a campaign to reunite religious ritual with the realities of everyday life by bringing God into people's homes, where people actually live and eat and make love, and still sometimes even get born and die. We need bishops who will walk round their dioceses if it takes them 15 years to walk from one parish to the next, from one rubbish tip to the next, from one casualty ward to the next, one mental hospital to the next, one supermarket to the next, one brothel to the next. Let the letters about drainage pile up, let the invitations to dinner with the mayor and to marry the Lord Lieutenant's daughter and to open charity antique fairs receive the priority they deserve, for while the bishops are flogging themselves to death keeping an antique bazaar of their own ticking over, the initiatives for personal involvement in the life of the nation, as ordinary people experience it, are slipping away.

Even initiatives for personal leadership within the Church itself are seldom exploited to the full. The present Archbishop of Canterbury will go down in history as a great ecumenist and an international champion of human rights; ecumenically, he has spread his arms wide in truly Anglican style, preaching in non-conformist churches and Orthodox cathedrals, embracing Roman Catholic cardinals and sitting in silence with Quakers. This has been politically wise as well as personally sincere. But during his period of supreme office he had an opportunity to overcome the easy temptation of enthusiasm for a cause whose sacrificial goal is at worst theoretical, at best a long way off, and to throw his influence behind a positive and immediate ecumenical proposal, the Scheme for Anglican-Methodist Reunion.

It is true that Dr. Ramsey did support the Scheme. But he went on record as supporting it too late, and he did so because he took the view, while other people were making up their own minds, or more likely were sinking into their own prejudices, that whatever line he advocated he would be accused either of failing to give a lead or of trying to steamroller the Scheme. The result in the end was that he made two brilliantly reasoned speeches in favour of the Scheme too late to two Convocations who had already made up their own minds. If Dr. Ramsey believed that the Scheme was theologically sound and the right way forward for his own Church and the Methodist Church, and was in the best interests of the ecumenical movement generally, indeed, that it was probably the most important ecclesiastical issue of his time, then surely he would have been wise to have nailed his flag to the mast at the beginning of the battle, to have said to the Church of England, "I have studied this Scheme, I believe it is God's will that we should accept it, I commend it to you for the following reasons", and then to have cleared his diary for a few vital months and gone round the country addressing diocesan conferences on the subject, confronting his own Church in public with his beliefs, and challenging the dioceses either to declare their opposition on spurious grounds or to produce sound theological objections.

Instead, he waited in the wings, which may be what sensible politicians do who hope to win the day by being politic, but is not what real leaders do who intend to win the day by personal example. Had the Scheme failed even after Dr. Ramsey had championed it throughout the land, he would at least have gone down with his flag flying. As it was, when the Anglican vote went against the Scheme in the Convocations on July 8, 1969 he took the decision as a personal affront, and retired for several weeks into a practically paranoid depression, even considering the possibility of resignation. There was a dinner party at Lambeth Palace one night during this painful period when all the guests left without Dr. Ramsey noticing, for he was so engrossed in a conversation with me about the failure of the vote.

Who is to succeed Dr. Ramsey as Archbishop of Canterbury, and how is he to organise the demands of his office in such a way that the considerable fund of good will still surprisingly enough held in the country towards the Church of England is not dissipated any further? My own guess is that Dr. Ramsey will remain in office another two or three years, and that he will resign a wiser but sadder man than he was when he moved from the north he loved so much to the cold comfort of Canterbury. And I believe he will go down in history not just as a warm-hearted ecumenist and a man who literally shrinks from the horrors of inhumanity but, like Pope John, he will be remembered as a stop-gap Primate; he succeeded an archbishop primarily noted for administrative zeal, who despite an under-rated concern for ecumenism did believe it was absolutely vital, after the war, to reform canon law! In my opinion he needs to be succeeded by a man emotionally unafraid to confront the world in the world, not from the safety of a study; by a man who is psychologically equipped to bring the reality of Christianity home to people in their homes. During the next decade we are going to need a Primate who is not just pastoral on paper but who cares enough for people to turn the theological colleges upside down so as to train a generation of priests who will cease to escape into the priesthood to escape from their own problems but who will embrace the priesthood in order to bring Christian insights to bear on other people's problems. And Christian insights are useless unless they start where Christ left off, hanging on a cross.

However, I am not optimistic about either the Church of England's ability to learn from its mistakes or its serious desire to attempt to adapt to the future. One of my reasons for pessimism lies in the methods by which the establishment went about replacing me. The Archbishop himself was left in no doubt during the course of private conversations with working journalists that it would be fatal to place my successor where I had been so uncomfortable, within the Church Information Office and between two masters, himself and General Block. This was a nettle the Archbishop firmly refused to grasp. He also allowed the Church Information Advisory Committee, in the interests of an uneconomic financial economy, to down-grade the post, resurrecting the title of chief press officer, as if whoever was to try to get the C.I.O. on to a respected footing again was not going to have a hard enough task without being 'demoted' in the process.

With time running dangerously short before the Archbishop was due to leave on November 12 for his tour of the Church of the Province of South Africa, he began to put out his own feelers. The man he chose and tried to persuade to join his staff was Wilfred De'Ath, a young freelance writer and broadcaster who would have been ideal for the post. But the Archbishop actually demanded that he should give up all his freelance commitments. Very wisely, De'Ath declined to wreck his career as well as step into the spider's web of political intrigue at Church House. Meanwhile, General Block's original five-year contract was extended for a further four years! There will, of course, only be one final solution to the Church of England's public relations problem; eventually the chief informa- tion officer must be replaced by a man capable of being press officer to the archbishop of Canterbury as well. To have to divide the two jobs is absurd.

As to the Church's ability or desire to adapt to the future on a wider front than the technical handling of its public relations, it will only succeed in doing this if it negotiates abandonment of ultimate state control over appointments to bishoprics, and either elects or appoints its own episcopal leaders. The Church will then at least have in a true sense the leaders it deserves, and presumably even wants. At present the intellectual and pastoral abilities of the bishops reflects pretty fairly the age of mediocrity in which we live. But some of the best men are refusing bishoprics because they do not wish to become mere administrative machines, and until the present bishops take a month's sabbatical together to look at the Church, to agree a broad plan for the next 10 years and then to work out a basis for carrying out that plan each diocesan will continue to struggle on maintaining church fabric while the spiritual life of the nation passes him by.

If the establishment takes a merely traditional account of the rôle the Church ought to be playing in the service of society over the next 15 years, it will almost certainly send the present Bishop of Durham to Canterbury when Dr. Michael Ramsey resigns. Assuming Dr. Ramsey goes in 1972, Dr. Ian Ramsey will then be 57, and could be expected to spend 10 years as Primate of All England. The present Archbishop of York will be 63, and with only five years to go before drawing his pension he could decently be overlooked.

If however Dr. Ian Ramsey were to be translated to London within the next year or so (the present Bishop of London can be expected to retire very soon) this will almost certainly mean he will not be going on to Canterbury, for the Church would never put someone into London for a mere two-year spell. Whoever goes to London while Dr. Michael Ramsey remains at Canterbury has obviously been overlooked for the top job; my guess is that London will be given to Dr. David Say of Rochester.

On grounds of seniority and capability, who else, besides the Bishop of Durham, might be chosen soon for Canterbury? Dr. Tomkins of Bristol will be 64, too old surely; Dr. Wilson of Chichester will be only a year younger than his cousin of Canterbury. Dr. Blanch, the liberal evangelical Bishop of Liverpool, will be 54 and would bring a youthful, unstuffy approach, but would only have been in the purple six years. It would be rapid promotion; probably too rapid and imaginative for the Church of England! Dr. Moorman of Ripon will be 67. If London is perhaps given to the Bishop of Chester, Dr. Ellison (he would, in 1972, be 62, which is pushing it a bit for Canterbury), then Dr. Say of Rochester might be in the running; he would be 58 and have behind him 11 years experience as a bishop.

The Bishop of St. Edmundsbury & Ipswich, a former archbishop of Uganda, will be 60, and might just be considered for an eight-year stretch if his overseas experience was thought to count sufficiently in his favour. A man with some theoretical claims is Dr. Stockwood of Southwark, consecrated in 1959, who will still only be 59 in 1972. He would certainly make Lambeth Palace hum; the administrative machine would hardly know what had hit it!

He would undoubtedly hit the headlines too, and while Dr. Stockwood would do and say many admirable things he would need the most professionally competent press officer on the market to get his message across with humility, and I suspect that Dr. Stockwood would regard himself as his own best press officer.

And so to re-cap on those bishops at present holding diocesan office in the Church of England, who would be regarded as about the right age when Dr. Ramsey retires, and not only the right age but equipped with roughly the right length of service in the episcopate, the field seems to be left with Dr. Ian Ramsey favourite, with Dr. Say of Rochester well placed as a possible contender, and Dr. Blanch of Liverpool a fairly promising outsider. If either Dr. Say or Dr. Blanch were to go to London in the meantime, there would, as far as I can see, be only two bishops out of 42 from which the establishment would make its choice.

In Ian Ramsey of Durham the Church would have a Primate who had not been to a well-known public school, who had had little parochial experience, who was primarily a philosopher, and like his namesake, Michael Ramsey, a don and a scholar, but with far less natural ability than Michael Ramsey to express intellectual thoughts in simple language. So philosophical is he that he will go round a point 25 times to make it clear — intellectually speaking! He lacks the disciplines of journalism! His churchmanship and ecumenical interests are virtually unknown.

In David Say of Rochester the Church would have a Primate who for some extraordinary reason was once chaplain to the Marquess of Salisbury, who was ecclesiastically a safe sort of central churchman in the tradition of St. Martin-in-the-Fields, conventionally ecumenical and fairly interested in youth.

In Stuart Blanch of Liverpool the Church would have a Primate who was decidedly low and might give respectability to the ever-increasing power and influence of the conservative evangelicals, who are said to have gained some 120 seats out of 500 in the new General Synod. They would not in fact regard Dr. Blanch as a conservative evangelical himself, which he is not, but knowing how the Church of England loves to keep everything in balance it is possible that with Dr. Coggan's candidature safely disposed of, a low churchman of ability like Dr. Blanch might be looked upon with favour to succeed a high churchman like Dr. Ramsey.

But must the next Archbishop of Canterbury necessarily be chosen from the ranks of those at present holding an English diocese? What about promoting a suffragan? What about bringing in a man from overseas? A short time ago I would have suggested that the translation of Fr. Trevor Huddleston from the suffragan-bishopric of Stepney to Canterbury was not beyond the bounds of probability. Like Dr. Stockwood, in 1972 Fr. Huddleston will be only 59. He has held a diocesan bishopric overseas. He is a man who can translate the gospel into modern terms in the printed word and on television. He is an exceptionally able debater and at all times a persuasive speaker. He has a burning passion for the implementation of truth. Unfortunately, he cannot abide the established nature of the Church of England, and to expect the present timid men in charge to take the exciting risk of placing a monk in Lambeth is probably too much to hope. The experience might in any case prove just too depressing for such a man of action unless within the next two years some serious planning is given to re-designing the primate's overall programme. And as far as I can make out, nobody at Lambeth Palace or Church House is doing anything of the sort.

This inertia in respect of the rôle of the Archbishop of Canterbury is typical of the Church of England's general approach to life. It still believes that time and events will move at its convenience. But if the Christian duty is to keep abreast of changes in society, and this means keeping itself equipped to serve the spiritual and material needs of society, then much more study will have to be given to the world in which the Church is operating. I do not believe the Church should pander to society's materialistic demands for the sake of appeasing selfish desires, but I do believe the Church should be taking account of trends in man's understanding of his own nature in order to apply theology to facts, not to preach it in a vacuum.

The next Archbishop of Canterbury will need to be a man prepared to sit loose to the pomp and ceremony surrounding his office, to sit loose to the Christian agnosticism of some of his colleagues, to sit loose to the claims of bureaucrats over those of compassion and commonsense. He will need to be a man who not only inspires — and retains through many trials — the love of those who know him personally, as does Michael Ramsey. He will need to be a man who can demonstrate to a dishevelled nation that ecumenism is desirable but only of secondary importance, that liturgical reform is advisable but again is only of secondary importance, that the intelligent redeployment and better payment of the clergy are priorities but relatively unimportant ones; that what he believes most of all is that the Church is really capable of putting into immediate and practical practice the gospel of love. And in order to do this he will need the courage to say boo to the establishment, and if need be, in addition to making speeches in the House of Lords in order to help improve the quality of life, gird up his cassock and take up his pastoral staff and tramp the lanes and motorways and industrial slums of this deserted land to show by personal example that in the name of Christ he actually loves the people whose souls are in his charge. He will need to be a man who fears gimmicks for their ultimately self-destructive force but who does not fear to be seen scrubbing filthy tenement stairs and working for a week in a geriatric ward and enduring the sheer bloody boredom of an eight-hour day at a factory lathe.

For while people rightly regard gimmicks as short-term roads to popularity, they still respond, as they responded 2,000 years ago, to the power of imaginative gestures. Charles Colton pointed out 150 years ago that man will wrangle for religion, write for it, die for it; anything but live for it. Christianity should hold a balance between the joys and sorrows of this world and the next, and what people want and need is not so much a faith by which to die as a faith by which to live. The Church will demonstrate the relevance between our human situation and our eternal life when it starts to put into practice the most revolutionary creed ever preached, a creed designed to change men's hearts, so that love and justice may reign. And the Church will only begin to change other men's hearts when it makes a conscious decision to begin to change its own.

*An article by the author called 'The Un-Permissive Society',
published in* Forum, *Volume 13, No. 2.*

SOCIETY is in a constant state of flux, and once you start trying to
pin down any particular period in a succinct sentence you usually
end up using a cliché; the present period is a period of the cliché
itself.

How many of us who now begin to detect the first signs of middle-
age were Angry Young Men in the fifties! And how many of us
assumed we had been so christened thanks to John Osborne? It
was Leslie Paul, the novelist and sociologist, who first coined that
phrase — as the title of one of his books.

Then there was The New Morality. It wasn't new, of course.
And now The New Morality has given birth to The Permissive
Society.

The Permissive Society is never defined by 90 per cent of the
people who chuck the cliché around, using it mainly as a stick with
which to beat The Young! If you belong to the-country-has-gone-
to-the-dogs-where-will-it-all-end school of thought, The Permissive
Society will conjure up visions of unbridled public licentiousness, a
climate in which decent moral restraints no longer apply, a world
to which Sodom and Gomorrah, in retrospect, were like Hove on
a Wednesday afternoon.

If on the other hand you do not see death and destruction all
around just because a few liberal laws have been passed you will
probably regard The Permissive Society as one in which you have
an unquestionable right to do what you like so long as your actions
do not harm anyone else.

But the really important thing about The Permissive Society is
not its definition but its character. After eight years of socialist

government we still have boys queueing up to get into public schools, the honours list is as long and boring as ever, the licensing laws still pander to puritanism.

On the other hand, after eight years of socialist government we have reformed the laws on abortion and marriage, made homosexual conduct between consenting male adults legal, and abolished hanging and theatre censorship. I do not necessarily imply credit to the Labour Government for all these measures, but they illustrate a 'progressive' stream of events running parallel to a reactionary one.

If there is an outstanding strand in all this mix-up, a hopeful sign-post for the future, it is I believe the liberalising of the law. Whether a law is good or bad, if it exists people tend to take that law as a test of right and wrong. The Sexual Offences Act is a good example of what I mean. Homosexual acts between consenting male adults may or may not be morally right, but so long as the law said they were illegal many people who might otherwise have thought out the issue for themselves took the view that if the law said they were crimes they must be sinful too.

Now at least homosexuals have a certain amount of freedom in which to make their own moral decisions, and those of their friends who wish to do so can offer support, friendship and advice without the knowledge that they are encouraging criminal behaviour.

It is this question of freedom which is really at the heart of controversy over The Permissive Society. There are 'primitive' tribal societies still relatively safe from contamination by western civilisation who have got along perfectly happily on 'permissive' lines for hundreds of years, wearing no clothes and feeling no guilt.

We on the other hand are a paternalistic society, building our codes of conduct on hierarchal pyramids, with the proles at the bottom and whoever is playing father-figure at the top. It is no allegorical accident that Moses had to go to all the trouble of clambering up a mountain to come down armed with a list of do's and don'ts.

So long as society remains authoritarian it is understandable that its basic code of conduct should remain fairly inflexible in application, but I happen to believe that the modern desire for freedom with responsibility is perfectly possible of fulfilment within that same framework of old testament do's and don'ts so long as we substitute for absolute values a school of moral theology now known as situational ethics.

Situational ethics says, for example, that while as a general rule it is wrong to steal, if your wife and children are starving the rule can hardly, in all fairness, be applied to you; the sin lies at the root of an economic situation which enables America to dump millions of tons of surplus food every year while children in Korea are dying of hunger.

Situational ethics are not very popular among conservative Christians who tend automatically to equate sex with sin, and the quest for freedom with a desire to behave irresponsibly, because the exercise of situational ethics means that you have to look at every action individually to assess whether it is right or wrong, sensible or silly, sinful or not.

For example, most critics of The Permissive Society seem to take exception to naked actors in the theatre, premarital sex, and the open sale of pornography, but apart from a sexual element these three examples of current practices in our society have very little in common. They are lumped together because for too many people sex is simply the root of all evil — unless of course conducted at night, under the bed-clothes, with the lights off, and between two married people, one male, the other female.

And it is all too often only in the realms of sexual behaviour that critics of The Permissive Society believe that freedom is something to be stifled, remaining perfectly content that people should be free to kill one another on the roads, free to beat other people's children, free to contract lung cancer by smoking cigarettes and free to advertise cigarettes on television, free to prepare for germ warfare, free to exterminate wild life and to destroy the countryside instead of preserving it for their children.

The whole thing is very odd, particularly if you take a cursory glance at history, for then you find that so-called permissiveness tends to go in cycles.

The strutting self-assurance and untrammelled creativity of the Elizabethans gave way to the masochistic self-questioning and puritanism of Cromwell's Commonwealth. Restoration comedy was as bawdy as 18th century life itself, a century which led to the decorum of Victoria's age. Then we had the opulence of Edwardianism followed by the ugliness of the twenties. Now our own preoccupation is with a search for values that have some meaning in personal experience.

By general consensus the Greeks were a genuinely civilised race,

95

yet they encouraged boys to run naked in the Olympics. For sheer violence Shakespeare's plays have never been surpassed. Charles II saw his niece to bed on her wedding night with a shout of "For England and St. George!" The truth is that in most respects we are a good deal less 'permissive' today than at almost any other period of history. And life is in some ways more civilised. We no longer send children down the mines, as our self-righteous Victorian grandparents did; we no longer flog members of the armed forces, as Wellington did — although admittedly we do send people to prison for 30 years, which perhaps is rather worse.

Contradictions in our patterns of behaviour abound. If the pendulum is to swing back again in a reactionary direction my fear is that, with the excuse of slapping down experiments in sexual freedom, those who push the pendulum will take the opportunity of reintroducing a reactionary element into the social life of the country generally.

And this is not to say that despite the loose and largely meaningless talk about permissiveness, life is all that liberal anyway. The impression seems to have got about that England is currently enjoying one huge orgy. I just do not believe it. Sex education is still in its infancy, the police sometimes use powers of persuasion in drug and sex inquiries that go far beyond their intended executive rôle, and the press is predominantly right-wing in its sympathies.

The truth of the matter is that sexual behaviour has been so damaged by fear, secrecy and guilt that only a mere handful of people are now gradually finding it possible to take the first tentative steps towards a sufficiently relaxed state of mind in which to enjoy themselves. If society was really geared to enjoying sex rather than equating it with sin, as our Judaistic-Christian tradition has taught us to do, there might be less restless, frustrated nights in matrimonial beds; less unsatisfying promiscuity for homosexuals and less unfulfilled fantasising, lying and deception for heterosexuals.

The hallmark of the reactionary is his desire to punish and to be punished; the hallmark of the liberal is his relaxed attitude toward himself and others. I believe we are all born to be liberals. But we cannot afford to be relaxed until we have faced up to and overcome our own feelings of guilt. The Church has a particular duty to welcome every serious attempt made to enable people to come to terms with their personalities, for the Church was founded upon revolutionary principles of freedom — principles all too seldom understood by Christians themselves.

There is no doubt in my mind that *Forum* is such a serious attempt to help people come to terms with their own personalities, and although the editor may be horrified by the idea, I think he is doing a Christian job of work! Whether the institutional Church, which has done so much damage in the past by preying upon feelings of fear and guilt, will learn in time that human happiness depends to a large extent upon sexual happiness, I rather doubt, for the Church is currently demonstrating a disastrous inability to understand and act creatively upon so many modern insights provided by the secular world.

There are, however, a handful of Church leaders and theologians who do understand what is going on in the search for a responsible use of freedom, and who can see modern experiments, for example in the theatre and in law reform, in their historical context. I am thinking of Dr. Norman Pittinger, a don at King's College, Cambridge, whose pamphlet *Time for Consent* (S.C.M., 4s. 6d.) is the most realistic Christian approach to homosexuality I know, and Bishop John Robinson, who has recently published a collection of essays called *Christian Freedom in a Permissive Society* (S.C.M., 21s.).

I would like to end by recommending one or two other books for further reading, all of which have important bearings upon a proper understanding of the historical period now labelled Permissive. *The Roots of Evil* by Christopher Hibbert (Penguin, 9s. 6d.) is a brilliantly researched and written account of barbarities in earlier times, against which the 20th century, for all the wailings of the Jeremiahs, can be seen to be a relatively civilised time in which to live.

The Other Victorians by Steven Marcus (Corgi, 10s.), an account of sexuality and pornography in the 19th century, is an equally brilliant exposé of our grandparents' hypocrisy. *Banned!* by Richard Findlater (Panther, 6s.) is an hilarious account of theatre censorship — which was employed originally for political reasons and is now abandoned, as indeed censorship in literature and the cinema should be.

The Anxiety Makers by Alex Comfort (Panther, 8s. 6d.) is a hair-raising account of the damage done by doctors in the field of morals. *Sexual Behaviour* by Kenneth Walker (Arrow Books, 5s.) includes a section on religion, while *Sex without Guilt* by Albert Ellis (Four Square, 6s.) and *Sexual Morality* by Ronald Atkinson (Hutchinson,

12s. 6d.) are two important pyschological and philosophical con-
tributions to the debate.

An article by the author called Leslie, *published in* New Society *on June 4, 1970.*

Leslie is 67. He was married when he was 27 and divorced five years later. He has one daughter. He lives in a bedsitter that measures 12 feet by 18 feet, in a Victorian house in Earl's Court with 81 bells on the front door. He airs ladies' underwear in front of the gas fire, urinates in the washbasin, and receives visitors in a tatty silk dressing gown, some sort of female under-garment, a pair of nylon stockings, and the sort of brown brogue shoes school-mistresses used to wear on walking tours in the Lake District 30 years ago.

Leslie has been a regular soldier in India, he went to a Roman Catholic public school and Sandhurst, and for 20 years he worked in the Ministry of Defence. Now he earns £14 a week as a clerk at another ministry. He had a nervous breakdown three years ago. He pays five guineas a week for the bedsitter. His earliest sexual recollections go back to five, when he says he got an erection reading about martyrs being tortured. At a pre-prep convent school he was beaten with a strap. From about seven he felt an urge to kiss women's feet. Then he developed a liking for high-heeled shoes. He had two younger sisters.

"I would have liked to have been like them," Leslie says. "I rather liked women's clothes. I realised this when I was about 10. I was doing a girl's part in a play. I was the queen. I liked silk, and I loved colour. I loved silk stockings, and I liked underclothes. I liked high-heeled shoes. I had a lovely pair of high-heeled shoes but somebody went and pinched them."

He describes himself at his prep-school as the school whore, and claims to have been buggered by about 50 boys. "I was almost like

99

a nymphomaniac, I suppose. Then, at my public school, there was nothing like that. I fell in love with a couple of boys there, but it was just kissing, nothing else. I got this urge then for discipline. The monks called it discipline. It's a kind of scourge. I said I thought it would be very good for me to have discipline, so a monk used to give me discipline with a kind of knotted cord and it used to give me a bit of a thrill."

Leslie's masochism developed into a desire to be beaten and trodden on. "It used to give me a great thrill being whipped, by men and women. And I liked being trodden on with a high-heeled shoe. That's why I loved high-heeled shoes. I'm awfully disappointed with women's shoes at the moment; I loved stilettos." He met his wife on a boat at Marseilles, and failed to tell her anything about his bi-sexuality. He says he was attracted to her because she was smart and good-looking. She found out about his sexual desires when she discovered he owned a pair of high-heeled shoes and a corset.

Although his wife has twice re-married Leslie has a theory that she was lesbian, and thinks that his marriage might have worked with more frankness. He says he regrets living half his life without a marriage. "I have a suggestion, for what it's worth. I think if a husband and wife swap rôles every now and then, it would solve a lot of problems. I think a lot of people would like to be bi-sexual but something stops them.

"I had a very funny experience last Saturday night. A woman I met at a pub I go to, a very attractive woman, said I'd got the most marvellous blue eyes. Then suddenly she said: 'Would you have liked to have been a woman?' and I said: 'Yes'. She said: 'Well, it's funny you saying that. I'm not actually a lesbian, I live at home with my husband, but very often I feel I would like to sleep with a woman.' I said: 'Well, come and sleep with me and I'll be the woman.' She said she'd think about it, but that's as far as it went."

Leslie's current sexual activities seem to be limited. "I can't get a bloody erection now. I'd like to be a wife to a male-type lesbian. I want to be the femme with a lesbian. She'd be the butch, the man-type. I think there is a possibility of this happening. I get that lesbian paper, *Arena 3*. I've got masses of used stamps I was saving for the guide dogs. I've got boxes full of them. I thought I'd write to *Arena 3* and say I'd help them with stamps if they'd help me, but I don't know whether they'd put me in touch with someone. There must be somebody like that.

"I write improper stories, pornography. The last one, I lent it to someone and never got it back. I love pornography. I write it on the office typewriter when the department people have gone and it's late. As a matter of fact, that's why I'm smoking. I'm trying to get enough coupons to get a typewriter. I can get cracking on a typewriter. You see, my handwriting's so bloody bad.

"I had a pal some time ago, an old boyfriend. He was mad on high-heels and make-up. He had me made-up and he christened me Daphne. I used to have to write stories for him. I never saw them back. He used to get so annoyed, and say: 'You must get a typewriter', but he never thought of giving me one. I've been rather neglected lately. I haven't had any fun. But this bloke I picked up in a cottage in Earl's Court, he used to bring two or three people here. They were all younger than me. I should think mostly in their forties. Once he brought a young Chinese boy. He was about 20.

"I make most of my sexual contacts in cottages. Touch wood, I've never fallen foul of the police. I nearly got caught one night. There were two other blokes there, and actually I wasn't with them when they shone the light on us. I was by myself. I said: 'I've only been in here a moment, I've hardly had time to pee.' And I think the way I spoke, they thought I was innocent. I got in first, and they said: 'All of you get on home', and we all left.

"I don't think anybody at work knows anything about me. If they did, I think some of them would be rather shocked. I hope I'm hoodwinking people. I would like people at work to think of me as a normal person. Actually, I'd like it if they were all abnormal, like me. That would be very agreeable."

101

A dialogue sermon preached by the author and Canon Kenneth Jones at the Church of St. John the Baptist, Hove, on February 15th, 1970.

Q.: You are a journalist and a Christian layman doing a highly specialised job for the Church. Tell me how the Church Information Office in London can help communicate the work of the Church carried out at both national and parish level.

A.: I will gladly try to answer your question, but first I should like to take the opportunity of thanking you for inviting me to take part with you today in this dialogue sermon, on the first Sunday in Lent, and I should like to assure the parish of St. John the Baptist in Hove what a pleasure it is to be in your church this morning. I am very conscious that our sermon is being recorded for the overseas service of the B.B.C., so I will try to do what most of us Christians in England seem to find so difficult; I will try to remember that most of what I say ought, if it has any real meaning at all, to take account of the needs and interests of the whole world-wide Anglican Communion.

Your first question is partly of local interest only, because the work of the Church Information Office in London is concerned officially with communicating news about the Church of England, but I should like to offer a general answer too, for the Church throughout the world has a very serious responsibility in the matter of communications, a responsibility fully recognised by the setting up in 1968 of the World Association for Christian Communication.

The rather prosaic answer to your question, as far as the Church Information Office is concerned, is that we exist to serve the boards and councils of the Church Assembly, the governing body of the Church of England — soon to become the new General Synod.

That's to say, we give to radio, television and the press news of what the Church is doing so that this news can be conveyed to the public. Of course there is no guarantee that just because we give a piece of information to a newspaper that information will be published, or if it is published that it will appear in exactly the form in which we present it. It is our job to understand the methods and the natural limitations of the means of communication at our disposal. This requires professional expertise, and I cannot think of a better example of the modern meeting of religion and the secular world than in the field of communications. I have not the slightest doubt that if the Church is going to take advantage of the opportunities open to it to speak in one way or another from platforms like television and newspapers, platforms which command millions of listeners and readers every day, it must enter the world of communications as an absolute equal, on a purely professional basis.

I have no time at all for church people who think the Church should receive special treatment. As far as I am concerned, the Church Information Office should be run as a professionally staffed, professionally paid and professionally competent organisation, or it should pack up and go home, because unless the Church is prepared to compete for space and time on a professional footing it will never be taken seriously by those who run the communications industry on a necessarily commercial basis. And if anyone were to ask for my definition of a professional, I would say that an amateur is the man who takes a taxi to a garden party at Buckingham Palace while a professional is the man who goes by underground, because he knows that if he goes by underground he will get there quicker!

I said the work of the Church Information Office is concerned officially with communicating news about the Church of England, because we are one of the Boards responsible to Church Assembly, but obviously we interpret our brief in very elastic terms. For example, the Executive Officer of the Anglican Communion has his headquarters in London, and if he asks us to be of service to him we are only too ready to help distribute news from his office about the Anglican Church throughout the world. And very sensibly, the Church Information Office was asked to look after press, radio and television for the 1968 Lambeth Conference, the meeting in London of 500 bishops from all over the world.

As far as communicating the work of the Church at parish level is concerned, the Church Information Office hardly gets a look in here, because on balance there is an almost inevitably predominant flow of Church news in one direction only — from the top to the bottom. The reason for this is a perfectly proper professional one; parishes seldom make the sort of news that is going to find a place in national newspapers. And even when a parish does do something really newsworthy, it is very seldom that anybody in the parish or the deanery or the diocese bothers to tell the Church Information Office about it. The short answer is that every diocese should have its own part-time or even full-time press officer, keeping in direct touch with the Church Information Office, and every deanery should have one person responsible for keeping in regular touch with the regional press. I hope that under synodical government the whole matter of communications will be one of the first issues to be tackled by the new deanery synods.

Q.: Even if what you say about lack of communication from the parishes to the Church Information Office is true, do you think the Church Information Office does enough to tell the parishes what is going on at national level, by way of conferences and so on?

A.: The conferences which affect the parishes in England most closely are the meetings three times a year of the Convocations of Canterbury and York and the meetings three times a year of the Church Assembly. Every meeting of Church Assembly is reported verbatim, and these verbatim reports are available to the public at £3 a year. After every meeting of Church Assembly the Church Information Office produces a digest of the proceedings, called *Church Assembly News.* This digest usually runs to about 16 pages, and can be ordered in bulk by a diocese, or purchased by individuals for a mere 6d. Meetings of the Convocations and Church Assembly are pretty fully reported in the *Church Times* and the *Church of England Newspaper,* and if the Assembly says anything of direct concern and interest to the world, as it did for example this month during a debate on the way we are polluting and destroying our natural resources, reports will often appear on the wireless and in secular newspapers as well. There is no lack of published material. But the truth of the matter is that people in the parishes are not exactly panting to read reports of conferences and debates, and I don't entirely blame them. I think we have become too dependent on conference reports; they can be a dreadfully dangerous alternative to personal action. It is far more important that people should simply be encouarged to imitate the life of our Lord — and we have no evidence that he ever attended a conference or wrote a report. *Q.:* While in your professional life you have the job of communicating 'official' Church news, so to speak, you must possess your own personal attitudes and beliefs, and these perhaps colour the approach which you adopt to your work. Tell me, for example, about some of the changes you would like to see in the life of the Church of England during, let us say, the next 10 years.

A.: Well, where do I begin! First of all, of course, all the changes I would like to see in the Church during the next decade or so depend on the way I see events developing in the world, for clearly while the Church will always rightly hold fast to certain basic beliefs she must never forget that she exists to serve God by serving man, and unless she takes account of the changing needs of man she will fail to help in the fulfilment of man's fundamental drive — the quest for truth.

There is I think a dangerously complacent attitude among certain Christians, who seem to believe that no matter how stupidly we behave towards ourselves and towards our neighbours, God will somehow always get us out of the mess. This doctrine, if it is a doctrine, is a denial of the consequences of freewill, for it becomes daily more obvious that man has the ability, and I am beginning to fear he also has the wish, to finish himself off. Humanly speaking, all the indications are that things are going to get a great deal worse before they get better, if indeed they ever do improve.

In England, certainly, there is a grave danger that the gap between society and the Church is going to continue to widen. For example, during the next 10 years I foresee immense and belated strides being made in the scientific and psychological study of sexuality in relation to the human personality, and it seems to me absolutely vital that the Church should tackle without delay the working out of a new theology of sex. To say officially that sexual relations are morally permissable only within the marriage of heterosexual partners is to beg a whole host of theological questions. A few weeks ago B.B.C. television produced a programme in the *Horizon* series called 'Sex and Sexuality', which I thought quite excellent, but I think the Church should be ashamed that not a single Christian was asked to contribute.

Then again, during the next 10 years I think the general pace of change is going to become more and more rapid, and in England,

106

at any rate, people are going to find it increasingly difficult to cope with the noise and the dirt, with the inhuman town planning, the destruction of the countryside and the general discomfort and depersonalisation that goes with urban life. To help cope with problems like these I would like to see the Church really emphasising the value of the spiritual life. One of the great hopes for the future is that many young people have already discovered for themselves the innate value of mysticism, and in order to help Christians to serve their neighbours more effectively I should like to see the Church encouraging regular retreats, by making it financially possible for all of us to find the peace and quiet we so desperately need, and which we shall need increasingly as the stresses imposed upon us by our largely artificial way of life become ever greater than our bodies were built to bear.

Another way in which I should like to see the Church preparing itself to serve mankind more effectively is by making a really determined experiment in community relations, for I believe that a sense of Christian community can only be built up nowadays in people's homes. We should be meeting together for prayer and for communal meals and for Holy Communion in each other's houses, and then perhaps we should find ourselves acting as human beings in human situations. Fewer old people would end up in old people's homes, fewer lonely, neurotic people would end up isolated from their neighbours, and dying would again become part and parcel of life, not the great unmentionable private terror now euphemistically known in England as 'passing away'.

Having prepared ourselves to serve society by obtaining some measure of emotional stability for ourselves I should, during the next decade, like to see the Church taking a really positive rôle in world events, forming and voicing Christian judgments on the major international social and political issues, and helping politicians to get their moral priorities right. For in the world at large I suspect that the next 10 years or so will see a major power struggle between the affluent West and the impoverished East. In a world of shrinking communications you cannot expect two-thirds of the world to go on starving in silence for ever while the other third continues to manufacture weapons and throw away surplus food in order to maintain its own standard of living. Of course, a parish in a prosperous, middle-class town like Hove is dangerously isolated from the facts of life as they affect the vast majority of people, but sooner or later parishes in England will have to wake up to, and act upon, the Christian belief that every man is a brother, or else they will have to declare a kind of Christian U.D.I., go it alone and face the consequences.

We need two things, and we need them quickly. We need a theologically educated laity, who do not need to sit around waiting all day for a lead from the bishops, and we need to appoint in the Church of England parish priests and archdeacons and deans and bishops from the Anglican Churches overseas, especially from those countries which in recent years have supplied the majority of our Commonwealth immigrants, in whose presence in England, incidentally, I rejoice. There will soon be a grown-up generation of coloured boys in England who came to this country as immigrants and who are now English citizens, and the Church of England should also be making speedy provision to encourage some of these immigrant lads to enter our theological colleges, or else we shall be missing the same sort of opportunity that we missed during the Victorian industrial revolution, and we shall again reap the same result — an unhappy isolation from the society of our time.

Q.: As an employee of the Church Information Office you work at the bureaucratic centre of Church affairs. Do you think that the government of the Church of England is relevant to the world or even to its own members?

A.: I suppose that all government exists to get things done, and if you take the view that not enough is being done, or that the wrong things are being done, then presumably the government of the Church is not as relevant as it should be. But equally I doubt if it is really relevant to blame Church Assembly for all our discontents. Whenever we feel dissatisfied there is no easier remedy than to find a whipping-boy, and rather than do something to put things right ourselves we say, "Oh, it's Them; it's the government, or the town council, or Church Assembly."

There are certainly two ways I can think of in which Church government in England can be said to be irrelevant. One is in the kind of membership of the present House of Laity, which nobody can claim is representative of the laity of the Church of England; here there is, I think, a built-in problem, which will remain in the new General Synod, for if the Synod is to meet for about four days three times a year, in London or in York, the majority of lay men and women who can get time off to attend and who can afford to do so are inevitably going to be middle-aged and middle-class. I see no solution to this problem. The other way in which I think Church government in England is irrelevant is in the system of Crown appointments. The Church of England is the only established Church in the entire Anglican Communion, and implementation before too long of the present proposals for Anglican-Methodist reunion would, apart from anything else, hasten the day when the Church of England would simply have to sever some of its present ties with the state. This would help enormously to bring the Church of this country into line with those independent Anglican Churches in the rest of the world who still look towards Canterbury with love and affection but with a certain very understandable measure of bewilderment!

But basically I think that any Christian who worries too much about the relevance or otherwise of Church government has got his own priorities wrong, because the chances are he is merely finding an excuse not to examine the relevance of his own Christian witness in the local community.

Q.: Finally, I'd like to go back to your own job. You are press officer to the Archbishop of Canterbury. Why does the Archbishop need a press officer, and what can you do for his public image?

A.: The Archbishop of Canterbury is the senior archbishop in an established Church; he is acknowledged as first among equals in the world-wide Anglican Communion, and when I travel with him overseas I see him acknowledged everywhere as an international champion of human rights and as the most respected world exponent of ecumenism; and through membership of the House of Lords he has political responsibilities to the state. So there is an inevitable focus of attention and interest upon much of what the Archbishop does and says. If the press is to be kept fully informed of all that the Archbishop is doing and saying in the many fields in which he operates, and if the Archbishop is to be kept fully informed of the possible consequences of what he does and says — and fully informed about all the subjects currently of concern to the press and the public — he requires a full-time, professional press officer. And I mean a press officer, not a public relations consultant. It is not my job to sell the Archbishop. It is my job to help explain the Archbishop to other people, and to help explain certain technical aspects of the world to the Archbishop. It is partly my job to set the Archbishop free to do his own job more effectively.

No previous Archbishop of Canterbury has been so open to communications. Dr. Ramsey is the first archbishop to entertain the press regularly in his own home, he is the first archbishop to be invited to address a luncheon given by the Newspaper Conference, he is the first archbishop to be invited to give an interview to *Campaign*, the journalists' own weekly magazine, and for better or worse he is the first Archbishop of Canterbury to employ a press officer.

So far as the Archbishop's public image is concerned, I take the simplistic line that every man in public life should be himself, so there is no question of trying to create an image for the Archbishop. The job is far more complicated, far more responsible, and far more interesting than that. It is a unique opportunity — for which I am grateful — of serving a very remarkable man, a man who bears many burdens, not least the burden of being a kind of universal father-figure. He is a man who needs and always values your prayers, and I know you will continue to pray for him as he tries to serve the Church he loves so much. The problems with which the Archbishop has to deal are not dissimilar to the problems which lie behind the questions I have been trying, rather inadequately, to answer this morning; how to change the Church so that it will meet the needs of a changing world, how to communicate Christian news via the media of mass communication, and how to govern the Church in a way that is relevant both to the secular world and to the men and women whose primary rôle as Christians is to witness to their faith day by day in their home, at work, in their parish and their church.

It is when I consider the basically mediaeval organisation of the Church of England that I feel most strongly convinced of the existence of the Holy Ghost, for without the aid of the Holy Ghost no organisation as creaky at the joints could possibly continue to exist! And it is when I meet individual men and women in whom I see a reflection of Christ that I believe most strongly in the truth of Christianity. For beside the Christian lives of ordinary Christian men and women, all the Church reports and all the Church debates and all the press handouts and all the press officers can of course be seen to be of hardly any consequence at all.